What Others Are Saying About Anna-Thea and This Book

"*Empower Yourself by Loving Your Body* is an inspiring look at a vital topic, and insightfully sheds light on the power of a positive body image. It offers the help and guidance to embrace your own beauty in all its forms. Anna-Thea treads on territory where few others have gone. With courage and eloquence she reminds us that loving your body is essential for a healthy and vibrant existence."

— Carolyn Krieg, D.O., Integrative Medicine Practitioner

"Anna-Thea is probably the most dedicated professional that I know. She is non-stop in her endeavor to help as many people as she possibly can, in as many ways as she has talents – and she has many. I was blessed to find her eleven years ago when I was desperately frightened and fighting cancer. I consider her one of the most important contributors to my miraculous recovery and my ongoing ability to better handle anything that comes my way. Bless her big, beautiful heart!"

— Christine Baron, Owner of Baron Art Studio in Las Vegas

"Anna-Thea truly is an empowered leader of women. She'll take you on a stimulating voyage into the care and feeding of your body, your heart, and your soul."

— Amrita Grace, Author of *Reclaiming Aphrodite*

"Anna-Thea is like a force of nature as she passionately encourages women to connect with themselves and love themselves at the deepest levels so they can more openly, authentically, and honestly love others. With its natural sense of humor and love, *Empower Yourself by Loving Your Body* is an exquisite reminder to all women; life isn't just about serving others. It's about going within and experiencing deep transformational change. It's worth the journey, even if the trip may take you out of your comfort zone at times. If you're a woman and you want to have more true, connected love in your life, then start by reading this book."

— Denise Michaels, Author of *Testosterone Free Marketing*

"Anna-Thea has helped me in many ways over the years. I remember dancing in the yurt and just letting go. I have attended her yoga classes and workshops, experiencing positive transformation each time. Anna-Thea is extremely loving, caring, and passionate about helping people. I am grateful to know her."

— Danielle Duffey, Owner, Silvermoon Graphic Design

"Anna-Thea has been a pivotal help to me in my relationship with my husband. She has open-heartedly helped my husband and me on several occasions using her own and very personal life experiences about grief and forgiveness. Our latest session with her was nothing short of an eye-opening, intuitive experience. I/we are deeply grateful to her."

— Barbara Berg, Singer / Performance Artist

"This is remarkable work, Anna-Thea; I clearly see your essence in it all. Thank you for bringing such important, provocative and essential wisdom to the world! We will all be FAR better for it! I celebrate you, your heart, and your Vibe!"

— Deidre Trudeau of The SheFleunce Factor,
and Co-Founder of Women's Success NOW

"Anna-Thea's passion and brilliance empowers women to quit just dressing up and dragging their bodies around and instead to love, nourish, and celebrate themselves, and ultimately, to take their rightful divine place in the world. Groundbreaking work! A big need in our society."

— Sonika Tinker, MSW, Relationship Expert
at loveworksforyou.com

"Anna-Thea has a welcoming spirit. When I first met her at a holistic networking event, I knew there was something special about her. She is compassionate, loving, and understanding. She offers a big heart and lots of love in everything she does. I am grateful I was able to experience her private yoga sessions (which helped me connect with Spirit and myself) as well as her teachings about femininity."

— Nina Lewis, Social Media Expert

"At a certain time in my life, I felt super-stressed, nervous, and didn't know exactly what was going on. Anna-Thea did some of the most amazing exercises with me. I relaxed, and intensely connected with my body. Between the sessions, I discovered that my stress was partially due to the upcoming birth of my granddaughter. Who could have thought that? During one of my last sessions, Anna-Thea did a birthing ritual with me. A day later, my granddaughter was born. For others, it may seem weird or ridiculous. I felt, however, the strong spiritual connection, and even though I lived states away, it was my way of supporting my daughter-in-law with welcoming her daughter. The connection that women have is a strong web, and I was blessed to experience this because of Anna-Thea! Thank you Anna-Thea."

— Cielja Kieft, Parent Effectiveness Trainer

"Anna-Thea's book is an essential read for every woman who is ready to make peace, or better yet, 'fall in love' with her body. It's for every woman who yearns to reconnect with her authentic feminine self as an expression of the Sacred. This is a most timely book that will assist and guide you like a trusted friend on your journey towards greater self-love and wholeness!"

— Isabella Price, Author of *Sacred Love, Manifestations of the Goddess*

"Anna-Thea is a powerful advocate and ally for women to experience the joy of feeling and expressing the potency of their true feminine nature. She inspires women to fall in love with their body and its infinite wisdom. This vitality is the core of your aliveness, from which love and spirit can soar to new heights. Are you ready to open to the gift that you are! Anna-Thea can help you!"

— Chick Lotz, The Pottery Poet

"I have attended Anna-Thea's amazing workshops and followed her informative blogs. Her new book, *Empower Yourself by Loving Your Body,* is filled with expert knowledge every woman needs to live a fulfilled and loving life of sensuality and sexuality. We were never taught these valuable lessons. I will purchase copies of her book for my granddaughters."

— Adrianne Carlino Gentile, Author of *Integrity in the Mirror: Wiping Away Your Fears To Reveal The Authentic You*

"Anna-Thea gave me the courage to speak my truth and ask for what I need by giving me the words to say and the direction of how to say them. She has loved me and helped me see that I am worthy to be loved. This has helped me to love myself and see my value. I greatly appreciate Anna-Thea and the things she has helped me to find within myself. I love you Anna-Thea."

— Gaynell Andress, Massage Therapist

"Anna-Thea lives what she teaches. She empowers women to come more from their feminine essence. Her focus on *yin* energy, which supports strength through softness, playfulness, intuitive knowing and confidence in this essence, offers a new way to *be* in our society; different than what we have been raised to believe. She provides women with many effective choices for fulfilling themselves.

— Nancy J. Boyce, Holistic Health Practitioner /
Therapeutic Massage Therapist

Love, Leadership & Intimacy

The flowering of a woman's sacred space
gives birth to a new humanity.

—Anna-Thea

EMPOWER YOURSELF

by Loving Your Body

The Woman's Guide to Reclaiming Yourself as Sacred

ANNA-THEA

AVIVA PUBLISHING
New York

Empower Yourself by Loving Your Body
The Woman's Guide to Reclaiming Yourself as Sacred

Published by:
Aviva Publishing
Lake Placid, NY
(518) 523-1320
www.AvivaPubs.com

The material contained within this book is informational only. It is not intended to diagnose, treat, cure, or substitute for medical or psychological supervision. Please consult your doctor for all medical conditions.

Anna-Thea
702-306-3984
Email: glowbal2@gmail.com

www.Anna-Thea.com
www.EmpowerYourselfByLovingYourBody.com

ISBN: 978-1-940984-79-7
Library of Congress: 2015901886

Editors: Jamie Gifford and Jeannine Mallory
Cover Designer and Interior Book Layout: www.AngelDogProductions.com
Illustrations: Megan Krieg and Kerin Lifland

Every attempt has been made to properly source all quotes.

First Edition

Dedication

This book is dedicated to all women on the planet. May they reclaim their feminine essence and let it be a blessing to their community and the whole world. May they feel the joy in their hearts by standing up for themselves and shifting to a new way of living and loving that supports their empowerment and sensual nature. May they be the leaders of love they are meant to be for creating the planetary shift needed to have peace on earth. May they walk in partnership and compassion with the opposite sex to create more zest for life as they celebrate their differences instead of struggle with them. I love you, women of the world. Go forth and awaken to all that you can be!

I also dedicate this book to my nieces and nephews, Christopher, Drew, Megan, Morgan, Max and Natalie. May their paths be one of love and connection. May they grow up to be loving humans, free from the sexual shame that keeps so many from their full potential. I love you all, and wish for you to live fully alive in your bodies on your sacred journey of life!

And I dedicate this book to my siblings and their spouses. They have been my cheerleaders and companions in my walk of life. I feel lucky to have them in my life as we journey together, growing older and wiser along the way. I love you, Bern, Caroline, Mary, Gerry, Carolyn, Keith, Joanne and Greg!

I dedicate this book to my late husband Murphy, who was my cheerleader and a big part of my path both during his life and after to support me in becoming the empowered woman I am. I love you, Murphy!

I dedicate this book to my mother, who was the mother all kids dream of having. She was a milk and cookies mom, and taught me the fine art of nurturing children, which has helped me show women how to nurture their inner child. I love you, Mom! Further, I dedicate this book to my father, who has been a strong, stable, loving and spiritual force in my life. He has supported my uniqueness and out of the box way of being because he has that in him, too. I love you, Dad! And to his wife, Barbara, who has been my cheerleader and open to all my unconventional ways of thinking. I love you, Barbara!

Acknowledgments

I can't overlook my friends, customers, clients, colleagues, book illustrators, coaches, coaching clients and anyone else I may have forgotten who has supported me along the way. I am grateful for all the cheerleading, service and support I received to make this book a reality.

I would like to give a special thanks to Carolyn Krieg for always being there for me when I needed her editing eye. Thank you, Carolyn, for all the hours you have given reading my material and giving your feedback. I love your sweet heart coupled with your brilliant mind.

I would like to give special thanks to Jamie Gifford for proofreading/editing the book and giving feedback. I want to acknowledge you for your valuable contribution. I feel blessed to have support and input from such an amazingly gifted woman!

I would like to give special thanks to Megan Krieg for the chakra woman she so artistically illustrated in the book. Megan, your talents run deep, and I am honored to have your artistic expression in my book. I am touched by the contribution you made to bring light and consciousness to our family lineage.

I would also like to give special thanks to Kerin Lifland for the other illustrations in the book. I feel fortunate to have such a talented and highly accomplished artist depicting my words and putting them to images. You have been by my side during the completion of this project and I am deeply touched by the generosity and focus you have given to me and the book. I feel tremendous gratitude in my heart for your love, support and contribution. I love your spirit and your pureness of heart. I love you Kerin!

I would like to give special thanks to:

Amrita Grace, Patrick Snow, Nicole Gabriel, Denise Michaels, Lorene Wilk, Jeannine Mallory, Leah Hopkins, Brian McCray, David Fabricius, Joan and Tomas Heartfield, Caroline Muir, Saida Desilets, Deborah Sundahl, Deidre Trudeau. Katie Carter, Zion Guinn, Danny Suffin, Antonio Diaz, Ulrich Soltau, Joel New, Alex State, Jada Fire, Betsy Gosselin, Gi Gi, Gaynell Andress and Teresa Brandise. I may have forgotten some names; if you don't see your name on the list, know that your name is in my heart.

Contents

Foreword

Empower Yourself by Loving Your Body is an informative and inspirational book for women. Anna-Thea is very passionate and committed to helping women. It was a pleasure to see how passionate she was when in the Divine Feminine Institute.

When I began my career I realized how disconnected women were from their bodies and how uncomfortable they felt with their femininity. What I discovered was they didn't have the tools and education to fully embrace their sensual side because they didn't have a safe environment to do so. This left them confused about the opposite sex and frustrated with their intimate relationships.

Empowered women are women who have learned how to embody their feminine side in an authentic way. They are women who feel comfortable in their bodies and can express their sensuality without an agenda. They express their sensual side simply as an expression and celebration of being a woman.

In this thought-provoking book by Anna-Thea you will learn how to be that woman. In *Empower Yourself by Loving Your Body* Anna-Thea provides practical, easy to follow exercises that support women to deeply honor their bodies, and to connect with the wisdom their bodies hold through mastering their emotions so that they can ultimately experience more pleasure in their lives.

When you follow the concepts and practices Anna-Thea provides, you will create a much more fulfilling life for yourself. You will experience better relationships, including the one you have with your body. You will acquire the specific knowledge, skills and wisdom to lead your life from a place of feminine strength and confidence. You will learn to embrace your femininity as sacred.

With all of that said, get ready to embark on a journey of exploration and discovery of how beautiful and powerful you are! I consider Anna-Thea to be a powerful force of change for women in the world. She has timely information for you. I encourage you to read this book and use it as a sacred tool to enhance the relationship you have with your body.

Caroline Muir,

Founder of Divine Feminine Institute

INTRODUCTION

Reclaiming Yourself as Sacred

For the survival of the human species, it is paramount to create peace on earth, to create a planet of love not war. This will be accomplished through birthing the Divine Feminine. The Divine Feminine is expressed through honoring the feminine principle, i.e., earth, motherhood, fertility, creativity and understanding the importance of love. The Divine Feminine is mystical, magical, sacred and sensual. The Divine Feminine holds life, all of life, as sacred. The Divine Feminine is within all of us, both men and women; however, the female body holds within it the seed to the birthing of the Divine Feminine. A woman's body holds the seed of divine love needed for planetary transformation. Giving birth to and embodying the divine within you is your part of bringing peace on earth. As a woman, you were born with this power. Now is the time to tap into this divine love for the greater good of all beings. **Now is the time to empower yourself by loving your body.** Now is the time to be a leader of love.

As a woman, you are a leader of love. You may not be completely aware of this, but it is in your genes. You are part of bringing peace to earth. You are part of bringing deep intimacy and heartfelt connections to the world. You hold this responsibility within your heart and female body. You may even long to cultivate more love. It is important for you to claim your place as a leader of love. The way to be the powerful leader of love you are destined to be is to empower yourself by loving your body. Yes, loving your body…every inch of it, no matter what age, shape or size you are. I bet you have become a victim of society, and either consciously or unconsciously, you believe you are not good enough, your body isn't beautiful enough and your appearance needs to change. You feel disconnected from your body. This keeps you from reaching your full potential, experiencing true love and leading your life based on love.

Do you believe you will never experience true love? Do you feel inhibited and negative about your body, and does it hamper your effectiveness in the world? Are you frustrated because you want to feel more alive in your body but always seem locked in battle with it instead? Do you feel fat, fatigued and forever judgmental of what you see in the mirror? Have you sacrificed work over taking better care of your body? Are you afraid you'll grow old and frumpy, where your only sensual pleasure is chocolate or ice cream? You are not the only woman with these concerns. Millions of women yearn for more. Desiring a sensual connection, wanting to feel open, uninhibited and empowered in your body, longing for an authentic, loving connection to another and wishing to feel vibrantly beautiful is normal and healthy.

If you could feel vibrantly beautiful all the time, no matter what your shape, age or size, how would you feel? What difference would it make in your life? Every woman knows she holds something special within her. What's perplexing is the fact that our culture gives women the opposite message. For example, messages that we're not good enough, pretty enough or sexy enough. Or that we're not motherly enough, career-oriented enough, or that we're too emotional. Maybe you received a message that you were supposed to grow up, get married and have children, when that doesn't appeal to you at all. In the work world, maybe you received the message and pressure to become a man in a woman's body. What were the messages you received? We buy into what society says women should be, and in many ways, we have armored ourselves up in order to be successful in this more masculine-oriented world.

I understand your pain. I have suffered greatly from all of the above. I found wisdom, practices and ways of living that helped me find my way home to a place of inner peace and acceptance. I gained tools that have taken me from anxiety and quiet suffering to a place of inner balance and a deeper understanding of my body and emotions. I have learned to speak my truth with compassion and set healthy boundaries. This has allowed me to experience healthier, more loving and truly intimate relationships than I have ever thought possible. As a result, I feel empowered in my body and can now be more authentic and effective in the world!

I have always been an extremely emotional and intense person. In my younger years, my intense emotions led me to needless suffering. If I was to lead a happy, healthy and productive life, then I needed to deal with my strong emotions. And so, when I was in my late thirties, I began a journey of discovery. I found a new path, a path of honor and reverence for my body. I gained Yogic and Tantric tools that transformed my life for the better. I want to share that wisdom with you in this book, *Empower Yourself by Loving Your Body.*

Have you over-indulged in food, alcohol or another substance, where, it seemed, you couldn't get enough? I turned to over-indulgence, as many of us do, as a way to numb myself from me, a way to relieve stress after a hard day's work. This kept me from having deeper, meaningful relationships with others. At the time, I didn't know I was doing that to myself. I just wanted to feel good! I was looking in all the wrong places. It affected my ability to have a healthy, intimate relationship with another. It created unnecessary drama without me realizing my overindulgence was the source of that drama.

I wanted to find a way to change that. I wanted to find love that wouldn't take me on a roller-coaster ride. I realized that much of my suffering was a result of my own intimacy issues and not feeling good in my own skin. Wanting to feel good in my own skin as a sensual woman, I realized I was looking outside myself for acceptance and approval. I was looking outside my body and to the outer world for validation. I never knew that the only way to feel good in my skin was to open my heart and let that heart energy move throughout my body.

Think of this book as a journey, along which you will learn how to empower yourself by loving your body. You'll learn to lead from your powerful feminine heart so you feel good in your body. This book doesn't take an analytical point of view as much as it does a sensual, nurturing, sexual and creative point of view. This book will change your perspective regarding what it means to be a woman. It will articulate thoughts and ideas about women, sensuality and sexuality that are beyond the realm of current society. It will support you as you discover what it's like to love your body and yourself.

This book will show you how to put more love into your personal and professional relationships. You will learn about your relationship with food, your body, your sexuality and yourself. All in all, being a woman comes with an inner knowing; love is the answer, not youth. Outer beauty has a short shelf life. When we develop our inner beauty, it shines eternally. I explain what this means and how to lead from this place of inner beauty. It's an exciting journey of being, having, receiving and allowing more love into your body.

I will share basic self-love principles to bring life suffering to a minimum. A big part of women's suffering in our society is that we live in a world that is not conducive to our flowering. I will explain why and what you can do about it. When you realize this and begin to give yourself what you need as a sensual feminine being, you will not only empower yourself; you will empower the world around you. You will be more vibrantly alive in your body because you will have reclaimed your body. You will lead your life differently, and inspire others to develop their inner shine by reclaiming their bodies as well. It's not necessary to teach it as I do; you can teach by example and by leading life from your sensual feminine heart. We need more women to reclaim their bodies as sacred and beautiful, no matter their shape, age or size.

Through the ancient and self-nourishing practices in this book, you'll learn how to awaken the divine feminine in you. I will show you how to appreciate your body so you no longer have to suffer from any level of self-loathing. This will empower and equip you to be the leader of love you are designed to be.

The Dalai Lama was quoted as saying, "The world will be saved by the Western woman." This is a formidable statement. I believe we will accomplish this as women release their armor and soften into a powerful understanding of honoring and loving their innately sensual essence. Western women are called to expand their self-love. This includes loving their sensual self and reclaiming the joy of being in their feminine bodies.

This book clarifies the source of many women's disempowering frustrations that often result from the disconnection and detachment we feel from our bodies. I support the reconnection and empowerment through presenting the concepts of getting out of your mind, having a love relationship with food, having a love affair with your body, putting more love into your sexuality and making a commitment to all of the above. I am dedicated to providing you with the wisdom and practical know-how to make this a reality for you.

Learning to feel joy and pleasure in every cell of your being as a regular way of life is my wish for you. I don't want you to intellectualize the statement, "Leader of Love," but rather see it as a path to embody this statement.

I want to inspire and empower you with an inviting message to initiate a positive shift in your perceptions. I want to inspire you to create new, loving attitudes toward food, your body, relationships and sex. I want you to feel more alive, confident and connected to your body.

My weekly blog, "Anna-Thea's Body Wisdom," is a great source for inspiration about your body as a woman. I am passionate about getting these vital messages out to the world. I'll cheer you on to love and embrace your body and be the leader of love you are meant to be.

I am here to help you. I know that there's a juicy, sensual, vibrant and empowered leader of love inside you, just waiting to express herself.

Are you ready to begin?

CHAPTER 1

Transformational Times

Loving your body is

a transformative act

Reclaiming you as sacred

a quintessential pact

You hold within you the seed

to create peace on earth

Loving your body

will allow it to birth

We're living in a time of transformation. The old paradigm, built upon a war-based economy, is no longer sustainable. The paradigm that worked for our parents and grandparents were based on a mindset of fear and separation. It is time to create a new paradigm, with new ways of living and loving. It is time to create a world based on connection, peace, and love. I believe women are the leaders of this mission. The purpose of this book is to guide women to become leaders of love through discovering their authentic feminine expression.

Since the feminist movement of the 1960's and 1970's, many women have become what I describe as "masculine adaptive." We've become men in women's bodies, especially in our careers. We have adapted a behavior of "going along to get along," often not speaking our truth and losing sight of our own needs and desires. We've adapted to a way of life that doesn't support our true nature. Inside each woman is a true "unadapted woman" who aspires to express her authentic feminine nature and sensual self. This woman is wild and free. She's sensually expressive, and desires connection and touch. Her partner also benefits greatly as she connects further with her genuine sensual self. She wants more love. Unfortunately, she believes finding "more" is outside her, rather than within her. I help women discover that what matters most is what's within.

Being an empowered woman, who also loves and honors her body, requires changing many limiting beliefs and notions inherent in our society of what it means to be a woman. On a fundamental level, this means changing what we think and feel about our bodies, our sexuality and our sensual nature. We're inherently sensual beings, creatures of love and nurturing. We often love and nurture others, but most women don't know how to create, cultivate and commit to loving themselves.

In the "techno-connected" world in which we live, we are disconnected from our bodies more than ever. We treat our bodies like rental cars instead of what our bodies truly are: temples that house our souls.

During our lives, the economy has grown primarily due to military spending. Unfortunately, the cooperative relationship between the military (and related departments) and industry is alive and well in our world, becoming more complex and part of our lives. In effect, we live in a war-based economy. Has this economy also created a war-based *reality* in our culture?

Many aspects of the world are about destruction in this fear and separation-based world. For example, we have the war against drugs and the battle against cancer. We have antibiotics to "kill" infection. "Anti" means *against,* and biotic refers to living organisms. Translated, "antibiotic" would mean "against living." Though antibiotics can be helpful, I find the word interesting and reflective of our culture's collective consciousness. Our medical institutions radiate and cut out body parts as a standard solution to disease. We grow up thinking this is normal, and don't know deeper ways of love. We don't know what we don't know. That is why our world is falling apart. Destruction, fear and separation are not sustainable, but they are built into our everyday life as "normal." The good news is that the old paradigm based on a war-based economy is changing because it is neither life affirming nor life sustaining. If we are to survive, it is time for us to create a new world—one that is life affirming and based on love and connection.

Guess what? This new world begins with *you* and your connection to your body.

Would you like to feel more alive in your body? Would you like to connect to it in a more positive way? What difference would that make in your life? What difference would that make with your body? What would that be like? How would that feel?

Experiencing more aliveness in your body is how you become empowered in it. To accomplish this requires a journey of being, having, receiving and allowing more love into your body.

Albert Einstein said, "Minds are like parachutes; they only function when open." In order to get the full benefit of this book, you'll need an open mind and an open heart. Read the book and put it through your own filter. See what works for you, and leave the rest. I know you will receive some pearls of wisdom to create a better relationship with your body, feel more alive than ever and lead your life from a place of deep, authentic love!

What is love? I don't have the full answer to that question. We are all learning about love. I believe this journey of life is a schoolroom, and the name of the class is, "Learning to Love 101." We are all learning how to open to love with each other and ourselves. I believe this is an evolutionary process. One thing is for sure; love is an extremely powerful energy.

What I have learned about love is that it doesn't require anything or anyone other than you. You could be in a room filled with people who love and adore you, but if your heart is not open, you will not feel the love. On the other hand, if you are all by yourself and your heart is open, you will feel a tremendous amount of love. Love is ever-present, a powerful and all-pervasive energy. All you have to do is be open to it.

RECLAIMING YOUR BODY

Similar to a beautiful flowering plant that is well cared for; our bodies come with natural abilities to express creativity, sensuality, beauty, goodness and love. Unfortunately, society and today's environment are not always conducive to supporting the expression of these natural abilities that are feminine in nature. They are abilities that are expressed so beautifully through the feminine form and female body. In a sense, our bodies have not been ours to enjoy. Our bodies have even been labeled "sinful." For centuries, women's bodies have served for others to enjoy.

A woman's body is the source of creation. We gestate and give birth to our species. We surrender our bodies to this powerful and important process. The female body has been taken for granted, and we have forgotten how important it is to honor our bodies. The idea of what the female body is has become distorted with a focus on outer beauty. The female body has been used for the propagation of the human race and a placeholder for men's pleasure.

Creating a new world based on love, connection and the affirmation of life is a journey of women reclaiming their bodies. How do we do that? By putting more love in our bodies, feeling more pleasure in them and speaking our truth from our hearts. How do we do that? That is what this book is all about, so I invite you to read on!

You reclaim your body by deeply loving and honoring it...all of it. This is how you make your body a sacred temple, by putting love into it. You've misperceived your body. You've inherited a number of habits from society that lead to unhealthy ways of thinking about yourself. You see the feminine "ideal" conveyed through magazine photos, TV shows, movies, billboards, love stories and all the other pictures of society-approved perfection painted around you. They become sources of self-criticism and self-loathing when women compare themselves to these impossible depictions of femininity.

It is important to be aware of the fact that you are bombarded with information, displayed all around you in society, that causes you to think you are not thin enough, pretty enough or *something* enough. This is the first part of reclaiming your body. Once you realize this, you can begin the process of re-education, changing your perspective about who you believe you are.

Most likely, you did not learn in school or from your parents how to care for your body in a nurturing way or how to accept a "non-perfect" body, a body that doesn't look like the ones seen on TV, billboards, advertising, etc. All bodies are unique and perfect in their imperfection. If you don't like your body, then you have been *brainwashed.* It is important to learn a new way of living. Making a commitment to learn a new way is crucial for reclaiming your body and regarding it as sacred. Are you willing to expend the time, energy and effort to create a more loving way of living with your body? Are you willing to own your body as if it is one of the most precious things in your life? If you are, then you will be greatly rewarded.

You will have the body type you have right now for the rest of your life. Your body type will never change. If you are short and stout, you will never be tall and slender. You can't change that. If you are a tall person, you will never be short. If you have big bones, you will never have a petite build. Your body is only going to get older (from a less accepting perceptive) and even less "perfect." You may lose or gain weight; however, you can't change your body type. We only get one body in a lifetime. We may be able to rearrange a few external things, but we can't change it very much. Ultimately, if you want to experience your body as your temple and feel empowered in it, you need to love, accept and honor it as it is.

It is crucial to know that your body, no matter what shape or size, is worth learning to love. No matter what our worldly pursuits or life goals, we are here to learn to love. This process begins with learning to love YOU. Learning to love your body is a fantastic way to start! Make loving and connecting with your body part of your "normal" life.

POWER OF THE HEART

As you begin to love your body, you must understand your own heart. Your heart is more than a muscle with four chambers that pumps blood through your body. The heart's capacity for love is not just a metaphor. The Institute of HeartMath has scientifically measured the electromagnetic field around the heart. They claim the heart's electromagnetic field is 40-60 times greater than that of the mind. To learn more about this interesting area of study, visit the Institute's website at www.heartmath.org.

The heart is powerful. It is designed to love. The less you allow your heart to open and love, the more your heart will suffer and the more the people close to you will suffer. Heart disease is the leading cause of death in the world. The earth is full of people who don't allow their hearts to do what they do best: love. We all suffer because of it. We open our hearts, but often keep them very guarded. What keeps our hearts from fully opening and feeling its healing power?

As humans, our consciousness is evolving. Every human needs a safe space. Then our hearts can open to love. If we don't feel safe, then we keep our hearts guarded. That becomes our natural state without realizing it. Your heart, when guarded, is like a metal broccoli steamer that has been closed and stored away in the cupboard. The good news is that the broccoli steamer has the ability to open wide, just as our hearts can. Every heart, even the most guarded, will open when given a safe space. For human consciousness to evolve, we must learn to open our hearts in a healthy and balanced way. We must cultivate love from the inside out. Loving ourselves is how we have love to give to others. It is not selfish. It is healthy.

The heart holds both joy and sadness. When we relate to those close to us by taking on too much of their pain, we don't allow them their own process for growth, and we suffer. It is always good to help others, but if we help others in a way that interferes with their personal growth, we cripple their emotional development and again, we suffer. This is known as codependency, and is not a healthy way to use the heart.

On the other hand, if you are rigid and keep your heart guarded, you shut off the free flow of love for others and yourself. Here, you must learn to master the fine dance between your heart and the way you express compassion. Setting healthy boundaries and knowing how to give of yourself without giving up yourself is important for cultivating healthy relationships. This delicate dance is how you empower yourself. You have an opportunity to practice this dance every day with those who are close to you. Loving yourself and others can cause you to lose your centeredness at times

Every heart, even the most guarded, will open when given a safe space. For human consciousness to evolve, we must learn to open our hearts in a healthy and balanced way. We must cultivate love from the inside out. Loving ourselves is how we have love to give to others. It is not selfish. It is healthy.

because we affect each other. You'll find that your heart does its greatest work in the balanced expansion of its powerful electromagnetic field.

Love is more than an emotion. It is an electromagnetic field, which permeates all of life. The heart's electromagnetic field is powerful and intelligent. Traditionally, we think the brain communicates and serves as the control center for the rest of the body. However, from scientific studies and research, we now know that the heart has its own intelligence that it communicates back to the brain. What is this intelligence? What is in this electromagnetic field?

The electromagnetic field emanates from your heart, then through your body. It bathes every cell in your body. It emanates energy to others as well. In the chakra system, the color of the heart is green (a more detailed discussion of the chakras is in Chapter 4). The heart is also associated with the colors pink and red. I like to think of the heart's energy as a bright, resilient, golden yellow sun radiating out in all directions—up, down, left, right, forward, back, diagonally—and shining its rays of love in all directions from the center of your chest. How often do you tune into this powerful electromagnetic field?

Just as people are attracted to sunbathing and feeling the sun's warm healing rays, when we "shine" from our heart, the powerful energy within will draw people to us. Everyone is attracted to this powerful and transformational heart energy. Our evolutionary process as humans is a matter of us all developing this beautiful intelligence of our hearts to a greater degree.

The heart is a feeling organ, whereas the brain is a thinking organ. The brain uses thought and logic, and the heart uses love and emotion. Love, and the energy it emits, is tremendous. Love is one of the most powerful energies on the planet. Love can heal. Love connects us, and love is what we are exploring in order to expand our consciousness. What is the strength of logic compared to love? Logic has its place and is important. When something comes from logic, it can be defined, measured and quantified. Logic is clinical and straightforward. Love can't be measured. It is mysterious, unexplainable, often hard to "find," fleeting or elusive. Love is far more powerful than logic, especially for awakening your body to its aliveness. It is an energy that will transform you to a higher state of being.

LETTING THE HEART MELT CONFLICT AWAY

When you approach a situation with love, it feels different than when you approach a situation with dislike, indifference, anger or fear. When you feel received by someone in a state of love, you immediately feel more alive. It has an automatic effect of opening your heart. The opposite is true when there is conflict. When you feel conflict with another, you feel constriction in your body. It might manifest as constriction in the heart or throat, or you might end up with a headache or feel drained of energy. This is real. Your heart's energy field is nourished by the heart energy fields of those around you. We need each other, and when that heart energy is cut off, we wither. It takes energy to keep your heart open, though I believe it takes more energy to keep your heart closed, hold resentments and not forgive. Unfortunately, many of us live this way. Could it be because we haven't had the role models or received the tools to communicate in a way that softens and opens our hearts to others?

Nonviolent Communication, a concept developed by Marshall Rosenberg, is a communication method that opens your heart. You can find his work on the internet. He has books and audios, and offers workshops. Nonviolent Communication will help you navigate complex, unclear and emotionally-charged relationship situations.

I was introduced to Nonviolent Communication by Tomas and Joan Heartfield, PhD. (founders of a company called Talking Hearts), two of my teachers when I was in the Divine Feminine Institute. They exquisitely role-modeled "equal-mattering" communication, a way of resolving conflict without blame. Equal-mattering honors each individual's point of view and creates a safe space to communicate from the heart, especially during conflict.

Resolving conflict in your relationships is worth it if you want to embrace your power as a leader of love. It will also bring a sense of aliveness to your body. If you often feel shut down or shut off from others, you definitely won't feel empowered or able to lead from a place of love. In order to be a leader of love and feel vibrant in your being, you need to stay open and let that heart energy flow.

It is easy to be loving and open when everything is going your way, but not so easy when you face difficulties in life. Love doesn't need love. However, life's more challenging and "negative" situations *do* need your love. Heartfelt communication is crucial in keeping your body's energy open and flowing. Heartfelt communication always enhances the energetic connection between two people. It enhances your vitality as you bathe each other in the powerful electromagnetic field of love and connection.

It is easy to be loving and open when everything is going your way, but not so easy when you face difficulties in life. Love doesn't need love. However, life's more challenging and "negative" situations do need your love.

When you can resolve conflict and get to the "heart of the matter" instead of staying in "story" with each other, you will energetically drop down from your mind and into your body or your heart. When you are in "story," you are in your head conjuring up ideas, opinions and often falsehoods regarding a challenging life situation. The stories usually contain some quality of blame, shame, fear or victimhood. For example, phrases such as "he always" or "she never" are statements of what would be in a story. These stories are a way of avoiding taking responsibility for a situation by putting blame on the other person. Listen to the stories you tell yourself when you are upset. These stories are not who you are. They don't come from your heart, and they will not enhance your relationships.

Your overall health and vitality benefit when you can consciously harness the power of your heart instead of staying in "story." It begins by learning to give your heart a voice when relationship challenges arise. This is where the rubber meets the road. Love and intimacy develop when you let your heart lead you through life's challenges. It takes practice to learn this new way of communicating and to incorporate it consistently in your life. It is similar to learning a foreign language. The next time you are in a relationship conflict and find yourself in "story," begin to bring focus to your heart. Don't be led by your mind. Learn to speak from your heart.

We can fall prey to getting stuck in our heads. We then tend to be critical and pessimistic. We see the glass as half empty instead of half full. The mind creates this negative way of living. Life becomes empty. Life becomes hard. We let our heads – not our hearts – take the lead. Conflict with others becomes a mental battle of who is "right" and who is "wrong." Such conflict leads to a downward spiral that is hard to recover from. It makes your heart ache, your body contract and your relationships miserable. It disempowers you.

Here is a simple example: A husband and wife leave home for a nice weekend trip to the mountains. They have packed the car and are traveling to their destination. They are excited about their trip. As they travel, one person says something that triggers the other. They begin to argue. There's tension in the air, and they're both upset. Maybe a shouting match ensues that drains both of them. Or perhaps they exchange mean, unloving words. Maybe they stop talking to each other. Then a silent wall stands between the couple for the duration of the ride, an invisible wall that has the potential to ruin their whole weekend trip. All it takes to avoid such a tragedy is for one of them to drop down into his or her heart. Has something similar ever happened to you?

EXERCISE: CULTIVATING LOVE

To cultivate love the next time you are in conflict, get out of "story" and drop down into your heart. Try this as an experiment and see what happens. If you are in a heated discussion, and you feel tense energy between you and the other person, begin to raise the energy by focusing on your heart. You don't even have to let the other person know you are doing this. Begin to bring all your focus to your heart as you continue being with that person. You can even stop talking. If you stop talking, don't stop talking in a way that gives the person the silent treatment. Just wait for them to talk, and continue to focus on your heart. All the energy you would expend to stay in story or to defend yourself will now go towards focusing on your heart. Direct your thoughts and energy into your heart instead of in the direction of a mental story that will worsen the situation. By focusing on the heart, you give space to the situation and energetically bring expansion to a contractive situation. The words, especially if you are in "story" and not in your heart, will only make matters worse. You will dig yourself into a dark hole of lifelessness. Let the focused attention you are putting into your heart work its magic. You may be surprised at how well it shifts the energy. Next time, instead of pouting in silence with a story buzzing around in your head, put all your focus on your heart. It can actually be fun. Consciously breathe into your heart. Feel it. You can breathe in, puff up your heart, and as you exhale, soften your heart. Or you can simply notice the energy in the middle of your chest. As you softly focus on your heart, it will come alive and expand. Continue to do this, and see what happens. Maybe nothing will happen, but you might be surprised at how it shifts the energy of the situation you are in.

Focusing on your heart is a subtle yet effective way to shift the energy in a positive direction when conflict arises. The biggest challenge is remembering to do it. Bad habits die hard. We are accustomed to being up in our heads, spinning out with stories that rule our lives with drama. We think we don't have the power to change it. We think we need to navigate conflict with our minds. Our minds will never resolve conflict. Instead, remember to focus on your heart when you are in a tense situation. Observe what happens. You will cultivate more love in your life.

YOUR RADIANCE IS A GIFT

You create love when you give your best self to another. I'm talking about your happy, centered, emotionally authentic self. I don't think you create more love when you give your depressed, negative, pessimistic self to another. Yes, even though love is ever-present, you need to cultivate love within you if you want to experience it. When you allow love in and surrender to that which is all around you, then you can give love to others. No one wants to be around a crabapple-type person. If you feel authentically joyous and bright, you will not only experience more love, you will also become a beacon of light to help others experience more love.

Your brightness is a gift to others. When you emanate inner peace and

You have a powerful gift: your radiance, the radiance that comes from your heart. Shine this powerful radiance, the good in you, out to others to lift them up. This is the mark of a true leader of love.

acceptance as you interact with people, you gift them that energy. Your joy is contagious, a wonderful gift to those around you. Good energy is contagious; we all need it from each other.

Unfortunately, bad energy is just as contagious, if not more! For example, if you are fearful, upset, worried or angry, then you are not giving a gift to the people around you. In fact, you might be dumping your negative energy on them. It is important to be authentic and real when you interact with others. If you are down, don't repress it or hide it. It's nice to call or visit with a friend when you need to get things off your chest. In these instances, however, it's essential to take responsibility for your emotions. Do the emotional processing necessary so you no longer hold onto dark emotions or let them lead your life. Don't make dark emotions part of your persona.

You have a powerful gift: your radiance, the radiance that comes from your heart. Shine this powerful radiance, the good in you, out to others to lift them up. This is the mark of a true leader of love.

WOMEN, THE LEADERS OF LOVE

I believe all people are fundamentally good, men and women alike. That being said, I believe women are the leaders of love. We can create peace on earth. Since, as mentioned before, we live in a world with structures based on the opposite of love, it is crucial now more than ever for women to take their stand as leaders of love and transform our world for the better.

We have all suffered from living in a world based on fear and separation. A world based on survival of the fittest; a world where showing your vulnerability is dangerous. A woman's body and her femininity were *not* designed to flower in this harsh environment. Our authentic feminine power doesn't thrive in an environment built and based on fear and separation. In response to the environment, our vulnerable feminine bodies have gone into hiding. We have had to cover up those vulnerable parts with "armor" for protection. Nonetheless, our bodies are designed to flower, to emit goodness and divine energy, and to feel pleasure. We live in a wounded, war-based, anti-ecstatic society. Overall, our culture doesn't support pleasure. We are more oriented towards pain and suffering.

As we evolve, we can create a world that is peaceful, blissful and pleasurable. I am not referring to hedonistic overindulgence. What I am referring to is creating a world where we experience deep harmony and peace from within. We can create a pleasurable existence, not in an effort to fill a ravenous empty hole, but rather from the feeling of fulfillment that comes when experiencing our true essence.

The external struggle we see in the world of politics, our economy and war is simply a mirror of what is going on inside of us. Creating a new way of living and loving that is in harmony with the earth and our bodies will allow the feminine inside of us to flower. We need to create a New Human.

THE NEW HUMAN

YOU, the New Human, are called to rewire your lifestyle patterns, as well as your relationship with your body, food, intimacy and your sexuality. YOU are called to become a leader of love and to embrace your full potential.

In his book *A New Earth*, Eckhart Tolle makes a very powerful statement:

"A significant portion of the earth's population will soon recognize, if they haven't already done so, that humanity is now faced with a stark choice: Evolve or die."

Loving yourself and your body is a revolutionary, evolutionary act that has far-reaching effects.

The evolution of humanity is about each of us becoming a leader of love. It is about allowing the power of the heart to flow through our bodies. When we allow this heart energy to flow freely through our bodies, we will experience our bodies as our temples and feel empowered in them. We will discover the sacredness of our bodies and evolve to a higher level of consciousness. In order to experience your body as your temple, to be a leader of love, and to reclaim your body, you need to feel good in it. To feel good in your body, you simply need to put more LOVE into it. You can even have fun doing it!

Loving yourself and your body is a revolutionary, evolutionary act that has far-reaching effects. It means shifting your body from a war machine to a love machine. What fun! It's about time! We have suffered enough. This book is not a comprehensive list of how to put more love into your body and become a leader of love, because there are infinite ways to accomplish this. The principles and practices herein will give you a great start in experiencing your body as your temple, feeling empowered in it and becoming the leader of love you were destined to be. Shall we begin?

EXERCISE:

In this chapter, we discussed the idea that we are living in transformational times and that we are called to be leaders of love. We are called to change our relationship with food, our bodies and our sexuality. Below, list five things you would like to transform in your life to create a more empowered, authentically feminine you.

1. emotional self mastery
2. rel. with body/oneness w/.
3. keeping heart/soul pure
4. confidence in own femininity
5. heal inner child wounds

CHAPTER 2

Getting Out of Your Mind!

Emotions... a powerful force
Part of being a woman... par for the course

Presence transforms your emotions to power
Making you blossom like a beautiful flower

In the first chapter we talked about reclaiming your body and allowing your heart to be a powerful healing and transformational force in your life. We talked about your radiance being a gift to others and that now is the time for all of us to become the new humans, living our lives based on love and connection rather than from a place of fear and separation. If we are to begin the planetary shift to peace that is needed for our species to survive, it is time for us as women to love ourselves and our female bodies. In this chapter we will discuss the importance of getting out of your mind in order to love your body.

BEING PRESENT

When discussing putting more love into our bodies, the first necessity is to Be Present with our bodies. Tune into your body in a completely new way, instead of tuning out or criticizing it. The past and the future are nowhere near as powerful as the present moment. The past is history, the future is a mystery and the present is a gift. That is why we call it the present. Being present with your body is one of the most precious gifts you can give yourself. It won't cost you a thing; it is priceless. The problem is that it takes time and discipline. It is something most of us didn't learn as we were growing up.

How can you be more present in your body? I like to say you need to get "out of your mind" because being in your mind doesn't allow you to be present. That is the nature of the mind. The mind is in either the past or the future. *Think* about it. Your mind is either in the past in *should have, could have, would have* thinking, possibly obsessing about "the way we were," or it is in the future, fearful or anxious about what might happen. Even if your thoughts are positive, your mind is never in the present. That is the nature of the mind.

What is always in the present? You guessed it – the body. Yes, the body is always in the present. If you want to be empowered in your life, then you need to learn how to get out of your mind and be in your body.

You might wonder what I mean by "out of your mind" and "into your body." A simple example of the difference would be whether you are saying, "I look good" versus "I feel good." If you think you look good, then you have a mental construct of your body. On the other hand, if you feel good, truly feel it, then you are in your body. You will never completely get out of your head, meaning *be without thought*. The important point is to become aware of how *frequently* you are in your head. It is useful to know the difference. With practice, you will notice when you are in your head and take steps that will center you back into your body.

If you want to be empowered in your life, then you need to learn how to get out of your mind and be in your body.

Perhaps that doesn't fully explain what I mean by getting out of your head and into your body. I will give you another example. If you are in bed in an intimate exchange with your partner, and you are thinking about work, the laundry, or are afraid the kids will come in, then you are in your head. Or if you are thinking, "Do I look good?" instead of *feeling* good, then you are in your head and not in your body. Being in your *head* doesn't allow you to experience pleasure in your *body*.

Another example of being in your mind takes place when you are overly talkative. Being a Chatty Cathy can be fun. We often become talkative when excited about life. However, unnecessary talking, what I call "frantic talking" to cover up uncomfortable feelings does not make for a sensually empowered woman. How much do you talk when listening would create a deeper connection with another? Do you use talking as an energetic way to keep others at a distance or to cover up nervousness? Unnecessary and frantic talking means you are in your head. The excess will drain your life force energy and disconnect you from others.

YOUR MIND KEEPS YOU FROM YOUR BODY WISDOM

An overactive mind can create an insane life for you. Your mind is not your enemy, though. It can be a powerful tool when directed in positive ways. It is easy to let our minds run amuck and create a less than joyous life. The mind is designed to see all that is wrong in its environment. That is the nature of the mind. It is a survival mechanism, designed to protect you from threats and harm. If you discovered a wild tiger in your house, you would use your mind to get yourself out of that dangerous situation. We typically don't have wild tigers in our houses; nonetheless, the mind is useful for critical assessments. For example, the editor of this book needed a critical mind to make it easier for you to read.

Though your mind is useful, it also keeps you from *feeling*. Don't be led by your mind, especially your critical mind. Your critical mind will prevent you from feeling life's joyous moments and juicy wonders. Become aware of when you are in your head. You will notice lots of chatter, story and negativity. You will analyze a situation, instead of noticing how it makes you feel. You are living from the neck up and shutting yourself off from the wisdom of your body.

Your body has great wisdom, and if you are present, it will tell you many things. The challenge is that your mind gets in the way. Your mind is busy with lots of chatter. We have, on average, 48 thoughts per minute and 70,000 thoughts per day! It takes effort to ensure that your mind doesn't rule you. It takes effort to get your mind out of the way so you can be in your body and experience the wisdom it wants to share with you.

Most of us live in our heads and don't even know it. I used to think we were a bunch of heads walking around. Imagine that! As I began to have more experiences with the opposite sex, I realized we are not only a bunch of heads walking around; we are also a bunch of crotches walking around. Imagine that...energetically inflated heads and crotches! This is often how we relate to others – through our heads and crotches. In other words, through critical assessment and sexual motives. No wonder relationships are challenging. We can bring these disproportionate energies into balance with heart energy to create harmony between the sexes.

BREATHE DEEPLY TO GET OUT OF YOUR MIND

What's the best way to get out of your mind and into your body? Your breath! Deep breathing is the best way to calm your mind, experience the pleasure of being in your body and feel the joy of being alive. If you are not doing some form of deep breathing on a regular basis, then there's a strong probability you are living in your head. This isn't an enjoyable way to live.

It takes a level of commitment to set aside a portion of your day and life to make sure you are not living in your head. The time spent is well worth it. You will feel more alive, less emotional, less stressed, more sensually alive and more empowered in your body, to name a few benefits.

Breathing deeply is effective for those coping with depression, anxiety and stress-related disorders, including eating disorders and obesity. Deep breathing gives your heart and lungs a good workout and quickly pumps lots of oxygen into your cells, especially those that may have been operating at a reduced capacity, such as the cells in an area of your body you dislike. When we are under stress, our breath is shallow. This leaves our bodies with decreased oxygen. A good supply of oxygen to our cells is necessary for maintaining optimal health. Deep, rhythmic breathing expands the chest, diaphragm and lungs, which invokes a relaxation response and massages the lymphatic system.

The circulatory system's pump is the heart. The lymphatic system doesn't have a specific pump. The pump for your lymphatic system is breath and movement. Deep breathing helps the lymphatic system do its job, which is to flush out toxins from your body. This will also help to keep your thoughts from becoming toxic. Deep breathing helps establish a more balanced and healthy relationship between your body and your mind. The best part is, there are no negative side effects to deep breathing. It is just plain good.

ADDING MOVEMENT AND SOUND TO THE BREATH

In addition to breath, the fastest way I have found to get my mind out of the way so I can be in my body is through two other important components: movement and sound. The breath brings in divine life force energy. Movement helps release blocks that hinder this energy. Sound carries the blocks out of your body on a note. You can practice breath and movement together. As you increase movement, your body will breathe more, and when you add sound, it further assists the process in helping to release tension, clear the mind and let your body receive a greater flow of life force energy.

Another term for breath and movement is *exercise*. And of course, we know that exercise is good for us. I want to emphasize that the breath, movement and sound component of exercise brings us into our bodies.

My first experience with adding sound to breath and movement (my exercise routine) was back in the eighties, when aerobics was popular. I lived in San Francisco then, and for exercise I frequented an organization that used various locations all over the city to teach their version of aerobics. The teachers were professional dancers who choreographed the exercise routines to music. At that time, they actually used 45's (a vinyl disc containing a single song) and played the music on a record player. The class included a warm-up, aerobic dance, cool-down, and arms, legs, and stomach routines. One song was for our warm-up. A few songs got us through the aerobic part, with other songs for arms, legs and abdominals. The company regularly added new choreographed songs to keep the classes interesting and creative.

Each class was a unique combination of routines the leader chose. The more I went, the more I learned the routines. From that, I was better able to execute the movement precisely to the choreographed expression. It was exhilarating. It was a way for me to express the "wanna-be professional dancer inside" without actually being one.

There were many different teachers. Each teacher had his or her own way of teaching the class. I was drawn to certain teachers. I loved one particular instructor's classes because I loved his energy. Only one thing bothered me; he wanted us to hoot and holler while we did the choreographed moves. I really liked him, and I liked his class, but I thought the hooting and hollering was a bit too much. I didn't get it. I thought it was over the top and unnecessary for civilized humans, so I kept my mouth closed. Nonetheless, I loved his energy and continued to go to his class.

One evening, after I had been taking his class regularly, I decided to go ahead and try this ridiculous thing he was encouraging us to do...hoot, holler and make whatever sound we wanted. I haven't shut up since! It was amazing to feel how much stress I released with each sound that came out of my mouth! It was as if the actual weight of stress was lifted off my body. I didn't know it back then, but I was making room for more divine energy in my body. All I knew was that I felt even better after his class when I included the hooting and hollering.

You may not be able to do that in a traditional yoga class or other forms of exercise. Find a place where you can experience all three: breath, movement and sound, and you will see how much more alive you will feel in your body.

Many years later, when I was getting my Kundalini Yoga teaching certification, I experienced again the benefits of sound added to exercise (breath and movement). In Kundalini yoga, music, especially chanting, is often used. It is not as common as other forms of yoga. Those who haven't experienced Kundalini yoga might even think it is a bit strange, because many teachers dress in white and cover their heads. Great things come in unusual packages. Kundalini yoga is definitely worth knowing about. It's not just yoga; it's a body technology for greater awareness. The certification program transformed my life for the better.

The certification was an eight-month commitment. I drove from Las Vegas to Los Angeles one weekend a month. I learned different beautiful and uplifting songs and yogic chants. I used my drive time to play the CDs I had purchased. I sang and chanted most of the way there and back. I released on a note all that was keeping me from being in my highest self, finding my divine nature. I didn't have to sing perfectly. There was no one listening to me in my car. I could feel my vocal chords opening and expanding in new ways. I experienced the release of stress through sound. I experienced firsthand how singing is good for the soul.

We can all sing, though most of us aren't perfect at it. Don't let that stop you! Open your mouth, vibrate your heart and express your soul in its highest nature. Breath, movement and sound will empower you. They are effective ways to be less in your mind and more in your body. It will open your heart, calm your mind and free blocks from your body. Being present in your body will enable you to lead your life from a more expanded and heart-centered place.

THE SIX PRIMARY FEELINGS

A big challenge of being present in your body is that unprocessed emotions can surface. How can you be present with your body if you are stuck in story in your head about life, love or any situation? Especially when something challenging comes up in your life, it is easy to analyze it and intellectualize why it is so. Doing this puts your body in a tense state. This leaves no room for Spirit or expansive thinking, and you start to "spin out" in your head. Life brings many challenges, and "spinning out" in your head in those challenging situations only creates more stress and drama.

When faced with life challenges, stop or slow down, and be present with your feelings. Many of us run from our feelings. For most of us, it seems too scary to feel our uncomfortable feelings, so we stay stuck in our heads, convincing ourselves how horrible a certain situation is, even making it worse than it is. We become over emotional. If you want to experience your body as your temple, embrace your full potential as a woman, and lead your life from a place of love and empowerment, then catching yourself and recognizing when you are living in your head, creating unnecessary drama, is vital. Become aware of when you are shutting yourself off from feeling emotions that aren't necessarily fun to feel. Don't run from them. You can run, but you can't hide from your emotions. They don't go away.

For discussion purposes, I use the words "feelings" and "emotions" interchangeably, even though there is a difference. Feelings are a result of your emotions. Emotions are a construct of the mind. They come from how you perceive things. Emotions are triggered from our thought processes and belief systems. Your *emotions,* in response to life and the world around you, form *feelings*. Feelings are not as long lasting. They come and go. Emotions involve changing our beliefs, perceptions and how we think about things; therefore emotions can last longer and in a sense become chronic if we are not willing to look at our beliefs and change our perceptions if they are not serving us.

Feelings and emotions, whether they are good or bad, have a tremendous amount of life force and energy in them. Your feelings and emotions can create both good and bad things in your life depending upon how you navigate them, consciously or unconsciously.

There are many types of feelings. For simplicity and better understanding of them, I categorize them into six types:

1. SAD
2. MAD
3. GLAD
4. FEAR
5. SHAME
6. NUMB

If you become familiar with these six words, you will better be able to identify and master your emotions. The first three words rhyme, making them easier to remember. After that, remember fear, shame and numb. In moments when you feel uncomfortable, notice that discomfort and attempt to recognize what feeling or feelings are causing it. You can make it simple by narrowing those feelings down to one or more of these six primary types of feelings. Getting in touch with these core feelings, acknowledging them and experiencing the feeling in the body are important. When dealt with constructively, they support your empowerment.

As a culture, we have become fine artisans of avoiding our uncomfortable feelings. Our society is set up to support not feeling our feelings. In life, uncomfortable feelings arise. It is normal. It is natural.

Numb isn't actually a feeling. I included it because it is part of how we cope in stressful situations. When you are numb, you don't feel anything. You are walled off from your body, power and aliveness. Though it is, in a sense, void of feeling, I include it as a feeling in the list. Of these six types of feelings, only one is good. The rest are uncomfortable feelings. No wonder we don't want to feel our feelings!

As a culture, we have become fine artisans of avoiding our uncomfortable feelings. Our society is set up to support not feeling our feelings. In life, uncomfortable feelings arise. It is normal. It is natural. However, starting when we were children, most of us weren't allowed to, nor did we learn how to, feel our feelings in a productive way. That is why people turn to things like overeating, overdrinking, overworking, over shopping, over sexing, over cleaning, over gambling, and more. We all have these traits. They are our mechanisms to quell or sooth those uncomfortable feelings.

You can stay up in your head all your life and not know it. You can let your thoughts and emotions control you instead of you controlling them. If you want to empower yourself and lead your life from a place of love, then you need tools to manage uncomfortable feelings. Otherwise, you will continue to stay shut off from your body through avoiding your feelings, building armor or creating a fortress to keep you from the joy and juiciness everyday life has to offer. Your relationships will suffer and you will feel a lack of connection with others. You will miss out on experiencing the full depth of sensual pleasure you are capable of as a woman. Finding the joy and sensual juiciness of everyday life and in intimate relationships is where the gold is! This armor also keeps you from being in a state of good general health, both physically and emotionally.

We learn to disconnect from our feelings as children. When we were children and got upset, many of us were told, "Don't feel bad." Have you ever noticed a parent saying that to a child? Or have you said that to your own child, a friend or your partner? It is from a place of compassion that we don't want our loved ones to feel bad. However, allowing them to feel their feelings is a better way to support them. Helping them feel their uncomfortable feelings and not making them *wrong* is a transformational experience that can help others and yourself.

Early in life, we learn to stuff or shut off our bad feelings. We received messages that bad feelings were just that, bad. In truth, bad feelings are guideposts to help us understand ourselves, and a way for us to open to love. In life, uncomfortable feelings will arise. It is normal. It is natural. It has taken me many years to not buy into my programming and to manage these feelings in a positive way. I experienced them so intensely; I had a bit of a drama queen in me. Instead of feeling the feeling, I would overreact, making a mountain out of a molehill.

Whether you are a drama queen or not, uncomfortable feelings are natural. It is important to know how to manage them in a productive way. Otherwise, you become lifeless, resentful, depressed or shutdown. You develop chronic illnesses or gain weight. You feel stuck in life and you aren't connected to your inner guidance. You don't have to live that way. There is a better way. Understanding, honoring and productively dealing with your uncomfortable feelings is the better way. If you don't, these feelings become fodder for making you feel lifeless. Having tools to navigate your uncomfortable feelings is necessary if you want to feel love in your heart and joy in your life.

The first tool is to allow the feelings. Don't make them wrong. Fear of "feeling the feeling" or being judgmental about the feeling will magnify it and make it worse. Do you deny your uncomfortable feeling by saying to yourself, "I shouldn't feel this way"? We haven't learned how to honor our feelings. That is why we often keep these feelings bottled up inside. Think of a time when you've felt bad and someone asked you, "What's wrong?" Was your response, "I'm fine"? You were stuffing the feeling. The statement "I'm fine" is usually a sign that you are walking down the road towards lifelessness in your body.

It takes a tremendous amount of energy to hold your feelings inside, and over time, they will rob you of your aliveness.

It is better out than in with these uncomfortable feelings. It takes a tremendous amount of energy to hold your feelings inside, and over time, they will rob you of your aliveness. The trick is to let your feelings out in a way that will enhance your life and not sabotage it. This will create deeper connections with others. It will open your heart instead of putting it on a chopping block. Understand, uncomfortable feelings don't go away by avoiding them or keeping them under control. Instead, they will come out sideways in what I call the "Three D's:" disease, drama, and depression. You could even add disaster.

If you are willing to feel your feelings and be present with them, you can transform them. Under an uncomfortable feeling is valuable information for you, information that will empower you. When you bring more consciousness to your feelings, they can guide you in a positive way to create positive outcomes in your life. If you avoid your feelings, they will run your life in unconscious ways, create disharmony, and sabotage your relationships, happiness and general well-being.

Feelings arise for valid reasons. It is important to acknowledge them. They are a powerful force and source of energy in your body that, when managed in a productive way, can immediately bring more vitality into your body. Imagine all the feelings you have pushed down, bottled up or put a lid on. Imagine how much energy your body wastes to keep them inside. Repressed feelings kill us over time. They rob us of our life force. They disempower us. Imagine letting them rise to the surface instead of pushing them down. Give them your undivided attention, presence and compassion. Give them a heart-centered voice.

THE "FOUR N'S" TO MANAGE UNCOMFORTABLE FEELINGS

I developed a process to manage your feelings in a productive way called the Four N's: *Notice, Name, Nurture* and *Need.* We all want someone to be there for us in relationship. This process is a way for you to be there for yourself. It is a practice worth learning.

The process involves directing your behavior toward what is underneath an uncomfortable feeling you are having. Though running from our feelings comes in many forms, I will use overeating as an example. Let's say you find yourself eating too much pizza or indulging in a second or third piece of pie, knowing this behavior will leave you feeling discontent in your body.

The first N is to *Notice,* "Ah, I am reaching for too much pizza or pie because I am having an uncomfortable feeling." You are bringing more consciousness to an unconscious behavior. You are shifting your behavior simply by noticing and acknowledging that you are overeating due to an uncomfortable feeling.

Once you take notice, then you can proceed to the second N, which is to *Name* it. At this point, ask yourself, "If I am having an uncomfortable feeling, what is it? Is it SAD, MAD, GLAD, FEAR, SHAME, or NUMB?" It is probably not glad.

Be present and feel into the feeling. As you feel into it, let's say, for example, you feel the feeling as hurt. Hurt is part of the sad category. You have identified the feeling by giving it your undivided attention, similar to what a child wants. To bring your body back to a state of emotional harmony, your feelings need your attention and love. Your feelings are there to inform you that something isn't quite right. They discharge when you acknowledge them in a compassionate and non-blaming way.

Each type of feeling causes a certain response in the body. Have you ever consciously noticed how fear feels in your body, compared to sadness? Or how anger feels, compared to shame? What does it feel like in your body when you are numb and can't feel anything at all? Sadness, for example, is a heavy energy, whereas fear is a tense or nervous energy. Anger is a fiery and often explosive energy. Become aware of the different types of feelings, how they feel, and how and where they occupy your body.

Once you know what type of feeling you are experiencing, you can proceed to the third N, which is to *Nurture* it. This is an important step. You may know that you're hurt, and you're able to name that emotion. However, if you don't go to the third step, which is to *Nurture* it, you won't transform it and you'll likely fall back into your old patterns of overeating.

To nurture the feeling, begin to notice where it is in your body. To begin, place one hand on your heart, and the other hand on your belly, or wherever you feel the emotion in your body. Begin to breathe into the feeling. Give it your undivided attention. This is where your feelings are, *in the body*. With your hands on your heart and your belly, you are literally holding the feeling. Then as you hold the feeling, begin to breathe into it and be present with it. Begin to nurture the feeling as a loving parent would. Hold your uncomfortable feeling like a baby. Ask yourself, "What is this emotion all about?"

For example, let's say that your partner yelled at you. You *notice* you are feeling an emotion. You get present with your body and are able to *name* the emotion: *sad*. Once you are aware of what the feeling is, you become compassionate and *nurture* yourself regarding this issue.

Then go to the fourth N, which is to uncover the *Need*. Under every uncomfortable emotion is an unmet need. With one hand on your heart and the other hand on your belly, ask yourself, "What do I need?" This is a powerful question to ask yourself when you are upset about a situation. It will help you stay out of story, which keeps you in your head. When you are in your head in such a situation, you give your power away. Your power comes from understanding what your soul wants to show you. Your soul wants you to grow, learn and live a more expanded life. Your soul doesn't want you to stay in drama, sabotage, victim or "stuff it" energy. Your soul doesn't want you to stay in a confining box constructed from limited belief systems. Your soul wants you to expand into greater awareness. Your soul wants to shine brightly from within your body.

Your feelings are the magical source for greater awareness. They can help you feel more empowered as a woman when you understand the underlying unmet need. Addressing the unmet need translates into more aliveness in your body because this is a process of learning to love and acknowledge yourself. It is a process of honoring your emotions instead of repressing them; it is a process of understanding your needs and caring for them. This is how you learn to lead your life from a place of love by cultivating it from within.

Look for what is under your uncomfortable feeling. It helps you uncover a core unmet need. Understanding your core need and embodying it is empowering. Your uncomfortable emotions are valid. Don't dismiss them. Instead, uncover the unmet need and either give it to yourself, request it from another, or both. It will steer you back to a state of balance. This process will help you understand yourself on a deeper level.

Knowing your needs and how to meet them is empowering. When I refer to knowing your needs, I am not referring to your desire to have someone change their behavior. You can never control another's actions. The only actions you can control are yours. I am referring to core needs. A core need is not saying to your partner, "I need you to stop being a jerk."

Core needs are normal and natural. It doesn't mean you are needy. Core needs are such things as compassion, understanding, clarity, cleanliness and gentleness, to name a few. In the example I gave of your partner yelling at you, causing you to feel hurt and sad, maybe your core need would be gentleness. By putting your hands on your heart and your belly, you are already giving yourself that which you need. You have already begun, by doing the 4N process, to give yourself what you need. Now, feeling aware and centered as opposed to emotional, and knowing that your core need is a desire for gentleness, you can go back to your partner and request that. When you do this, you help prevent unnecessary drama in your relationships.

You definitely won't get your core need for gentleness met if you say to your partner, "You are such a jerk for yelling at me. Don't do it again." INSTEAD, when you uncover your core need and embody it, meaning you feel you deserve it, and you own the statement "I need gentleness," you can say to your partner, "Honey, when you yelled at me, it really hurt. I felt sad. What I need is gentleness. Would you be willing to be gentler with me in the future?" Your partner may not be perfect, however, with this type of request, they will probably do their best to be more gentle with you in the future.

This type of request will only work if you mean it, embody it and speak it from your heart. The Four N's will help you develop a more compassionate relationship with yourself. Once you have discovered your core need, you then must believe you deserve to have that core need met, 100 percent. If you don't feel you deserve it, then your request will not come from your heart; it will come from your head. You may request to be treated gently, but you can't convince another person to be gentle with you if you don't believe you are worthy of it. That is what I mean by embodying and feeling deserving of your core need. When you do this, your whole being becomes empowered. Your energy isn't scattered or confused; it is centered and stable. When you "people-please" to the detriment of your needs, it weakens your life force energy.

Another important aspect of staying centered, stable, and empowered in your body is to use "I" statements when communicating. Using "I" statements instead of "you" statements keeps your energy contained. It is a way to communicate clearly and without blame. Assertive and authentic communication uses "I" statements. It's not selfish and doesn't mean you care only about yourself. "I" statements are direct and honest. "I" statements show that you are taking responsibility for how you feel. You are not blaming your partner for your feelings. "I" statements are factual and non-judgmental. For example, "I feel hurt" is an "I" statement, as opposed to saying, "You hurt me," which is a "you" statement.

"You" is not a negative word, however, when used to victimize, judge and control as in the statement, "You hurt me" (instead of saying "I feel hurt"), your words become an attack that doesn't nurture connection. You place the blame on the other person for causing your feelings. In that phrase, you are not taking responsibility for your feelings. From this perspective, "you" statements are more self-centered than "I" statements. Be aware of this when you communicate with others.

Use the 4N process any time you have an uncomfortable feeling. My one-on-one coaching often involves helping women fully understand and embrace this process to enhance their intimate relationships. I will say it again: old habits die hard. You may do it and then slip and not do it. You may not fully understand how to do it. I am here to help. Don't beat yourself up if you don't process your emotions productively every time. You are human, learning a new way of living and loving. Though opening to love is a lifelong process, this way of communicating has immediate positive results.

Remember to put your hands on your heart and belly when you are upset. Learn to be there for yourself so you won't create unnecessary drama in your relationships. You will come to your senses by sensing into your body (not your mind) when emotions arise. When you speak your feelings, remember to use "I" statements instead of "you" statements to take full responsibility for your feelings.

When you practice this new way of communicating with yourself and others, you will feel less heaviness in your body. This type of communication "technique" is not really a technique, because if you are not in your heart, it won't work. It is a way of learning how to give your heart and body – instead of your mind – a voice.

EXERCISE:

In this chapter, we explored needs and feelings. Knowing your needs, and how to get them met, is empowering. Set aside ten minutes or more, then get centered by taking a few breaths. In the space below, write down ten of your core needs. Remember, core needs don't involve making someone else do something such as, "I need my husband to help with the housework." Instead, a core need in that situation could be a need for cleanliness. Other core needs, for example, might be gentleness, connection, patience and support.

1. I need love
2. I need loyalty/connection
3. I need dedication
4. I need communication
5. I need clarity
6. I need sincerity
7. I need patience
8. I need integrity
9. I need strength
10. I need compassion/nurture

CHAPTER 3

Having A Love Relationship With Food

Food...a form of sensuality
When in excess creates a miserable reality

Let food be love going deep into your being
Expanding your essence, your brilliance and intuitive seeing

Allow it to nurture you deep within
Supporting you to feel sensually alive in your skin

In the previous chapter, we talked about how important it is to get out of your mind and be present in your body. We talked about the challenges of being present in the body to identify the source of uncomfortable feelings, and how to manage them productively. In this chapter, I offer new perspectives on your relationship with food, emotions and sensuality. I would like to help you create a love relationship with food as a way to further empower yourself as a woman.

What type of relationship do you have with food? How does food make you feel? Are you emotionally attached to food that isn't healthy for you? Do you beat yourself up after eating? Do you eat on the run, in the car? Do you eat without paying attention to what you're doing? What would it take to love yourself enough to have a life-affirming love relationship with food?

BECOMING A COSMIC BLOOM

When I was nineteen years old, I took a nutrition class in college. This class was a turning point for me, a key starting point for my long journey to learn how to make love with food. At that point, I was going to college; however, I had no idea what I wanted to major in. The nutrition class sounded interesting, so I signed up. I also had an interest in the subject because since puberty, I struggled with body image issues and food obsessions. I wanted a "perfect" skinny body, flat stomach and thinner legs. I obsessed about food while trying to lose weight. This led to a roller-coaster type lifestyle of overeating and under-eating. I also used food to quell and repress my emotions; though at the time I was unaware of it. I was about twenty pounds overweight, the most I had ever weighed. I did not feel good about my body or my relationship with food, and battled with both. I was drawn to the class on nutrition in an effort to make peace with food.

The instructor was an older woman, probably in her late fifties, with lots of energy. She was bright, cheery, and entered the room snacking on a carrot. I remember her telling us she hung out with young women on the beach. She was the picture of eternal youth. She made a big impression on me.

The biggest thing she taught me was about our relationship with food. I remember her excitement about the subject of nutrition. With great zest, she told us that we were all "Cosmic Blooms." She explained that when we take food into our bodies, we make love to it, and then we let it go. She said if we make love to it, why would we want to put something into our bodies that was bad for us? In other words, why make love to something that is awful? When she explained this idea, a light went on in me. What she said may have been extreme, but it was just what I needed to hear. It made sense to me.

Because I suffered with food, body image and weight issues, I knew this idea was my salvation. If I could shift my attitude about food, making love to it, not war, then I knew my world would change. I knew my suffering would go away and I would no longer struggle with food. She showed me the light at the end of the tunnel.

During that course, I realized what I wanted to major in. I decided to go to San Francisco State University and get a Bachelor's degree in dietetics. I was excited about learning more about this subject. My primary motivation was to make peace with food. Four years later, I graduated with honors. That was just the beginning of my journey to learn how to make love with food.

MAKING LOVE WITH FOOD

What do I mean by "making love with food" or "having a love relationship with food"? I am not talking about a love-hate relationship with food. That creates a roller-coaster ride with food, and is extremely hard on your body. You overindulge in the sensual delights of food and stuff yourself. Then you hate it, and don't want to have anything to do with it, because it made you feel so uncomfortable.

When I talk about having a love relationship with food, I am referring to making peace with food. I want you to think of food as a nurturing, supportive, joyous part of your life. I don't want food to be something you obsess about, control, measure, regulate, limit or overindulge in. You need food to nourish your body so it will function optimally. When you bring food into balance, you can enjoy it and reap the sensual and nutritional benefits it provides. Bringing food into balance is the only way you will feel empowered in your body.

When you eat too much of something that tantalizes your taste buds, you lose the ability to fully enjoy it. For example, a third or fourth "out of this world tasty" cookie never tastes as scrumptious as the first one. If you are reaching for a third or fourth cookie, you are having an uncomfortable feeling. You might say it is habit. However, uncomfortable feelings become habits too. Discomfort and quelling your discomfort become the norm. Thus, overeating becomes a way of life. Your body certainly doesn't need all that food. Though we can't go without food, most of us eat more than we need to sustain the body. This may be because eating is a pleasurable experience. Use the Four N's discussed in the "Be Present" section. Find out what is going on and why you use food to quell those uncomfortable feelings. This is a good way to bring your relationship with food into balance.

We are creatures of habit. If food is your way to numb out or sooth uncomfortable feelings, you develop pathways in the brain to support that behavior. I see these pathways as freeways in the brain. They aren't little country roads or skinny hiking trails. They are large multi-lane freeway systems in your brain that tell you eating lots of food is the answer to your problems.

Part of creating a love relationship with food is to rebuild these freeways in your mind. Make detours, and build new roads and highways designed and developed around healthy behaviors. The old roads, those big freeways, will never go away. However, you will begin to travel less on them. As you use the new roads more frequently, they will become bigger and more familiar to you.

What this means, for example, is that although you may have overeaten as a way of dealing with stress, you might not eat as much as you used to because now you have replaced your overeating with a weekly yoga program. Or you have replaced overeating with getting a massage on a regular basis. You are creating new pathways in your brain that give you positive sensual feedback. The new roads you've created become bigger, and the life-enhancing behavior becomes more frequent and more desirable than the life-robbing behavior.

SAD NUTRITION VERSUS HAPPY NUTRITION

Let's look at some basic things you can do to create a love relationship with food and build those new pathways. First, choose whether you want to be SAD or HAPPY. They are acronyms for two different types of diets you can choose. SAD stands for Standard American Diet. HAPPY stands for Healthy Aware Person, Purifying Yourself. I also like to say HAPPY stands for Healthy Aware Person, Perceiving Yourself. When you can perceive yourself on a deeper level and feel your vitality, joy, and how amazing you are, you will become aware of the divine energy coursing through your body. This leads to general well-being, or you being HAPPY.

If you want to be SAD, eat the Standard American Diet of packaged and processed foods. How often do you eat at a fast food restaurant? Do you eat organic food? How much meat do you eat—especially meat that is not organic? How much processed sugar do you consume? Do you drink coffee or alcohol, and to what extent?

If you want to be SAD, eat the Standard American Diet of packaged and processed foods.

Our standard food supply has become toxic. Our society is going through a health crisis. We may live longer, but we must ask ourselves if it is a life of quality. Cancer, heart disease, diabetes, obesity, inflammation and other degenerative diseases are on the rise. This may be an indication that there is something out of balance in our modern lifestyle. Getting ahead materially has become more important than our spiritual development. This is seductively depicted in the corporate culture we now live in, with all of its media and advertising.

Some of the largest corporate entities are in the pharmaceutical industry. As they profit, we get sicker. Increased consumption of pharmaceuticals may allow us to live without symptoms, but the imbalance still exists in our bodies. To imagine how pharmaceutical drugs work, think about when your car's oil light comes on. What do you do? Do you put a piece of duct tape over the dashboard? The light goes away, but the problem doesn't. If you don't put oil in your car, soon it will stop running. You didn't fix the cause, just the symptom. It is important to be aware of this if you want to feel alive and empowered in your body. An underlying problem isn't being addressed.

Pharmaceuticals have value. They help many people. However, addressing the underlying cause is critical to our health, and our society prefers to cover up symptoms with a pill. Sometimes for immediate relief, deciding to take a prescription medication is a good choice. Over the long haul, as a lifestyle, it has the risk of disconnecting you from your body. Being aware of this and doing what you can to be as drug free as possible is a good policy, though not always doable for many.

The point is we have a "quick fix" mentality in our society that disconnects us from our body. This isn't to say all pharmaceuticals are bad, but their use has gotten out of hand. Some of the most frequently prescribed medications are antidepressants and painkillers. We are a sad society, with people who suffer from physical pain, much of which can be relieved through a better diet and lifestyle.

If we are to survive this health crisis, we need to reclaim our divine essence by recognizing the beauty of our body and its ability to be in a state of perfect health if we give it what it needs. Your body needs love. It needs proper fuel for the mind, body and spirit. Doing this takes education, effort and even expense. It takes being committed to eating in a way that most others don't eat and possibly standing out in social situations. That is one reason why the quick fix is so appealing.

Gaining back our health is a complex problem in our society. We closely associate food with socializing and connecting with others. If you want to be with others and they are not into healthy eating, it can be challenging. Drinking alcohol to toast the bride and groom at a wedding, or eating sugary foods such as a cake for someone's birthday celebration are "normal" ways we celebrate. It is a double-edged sword for those suffering from food obsessions: staying connected to people you love, and not being challenged by having to be around foods that trigger you. I will always love a big piece of carrot cake, but is it good for me? Can I love myself enough to enjoy a small piece or a few bites, as opposed to the larger portion my taste buds want? Ask yourself the same question for those foods that trigger you.

If you have food issues, socializing becomes similar to a recovering alcoholic hanging out with his alcoholic friends in a bar. You need to have the willpower of God to expose yourself to such environments. Building the new brain pathways before-mentioned is helpful. If you find it hard not to obsess about food in social situations, make new pathways of connection. Next time you are planning to go to a social event where you know you will be triggered by the food, set an intention to shift your behavior. Before you arrive, set an intention for connection, as opposed to culinary delight. Make it your priority to connect with people instead of obsess about food. Don't position yourself near the food. Make eye contact with the people you talk with, listen attentively to them, ask questions and open your heart to them. This can be fun. Use your ability to obsess in a positive direction; obsess about being connected and present with people. Be there for them energetically. Observe them as though it is an assignment from your psychology class. If you begin to obsess about food, go back to your intention to connect with people and give them your undivided attention.

You will walk away from the event feeling more love, and you won't wake up the next morning regretting having had too much food or alcohol. You will have widened a new, healthy pathway in your brain. You may not be perfect in this new pathway. Give yourself a break and be gentle on yourself if you can't execute this practice perfectly. Even imperfectly, mindfully attempting this practice will help to reduce your food obsession and to open your heart.

I didn't say that having a HAPPY (Healthy Aware Person, Purifying or Perceiving Yourself) diet would always be easy. Maintaining your vitality in a world that is structured to rob you of it takes commitment and self-love. Convenience foods, processed foods, inexpensive buffets and the like have become a way of life for many. When traveling through airports or away from home, it becomes a challenge to eat healthy. It is not easy to find healthy food when you are away from home unless you go to a health food grocery store. This is changing, and we are beginning to find more healthy choices. However, we still have a long way to go.

The SAD, "All-American" way of life is dying. You can die with it or choose to be HAPPY. Food is the fastest way to change your consciousness. Food affects your moods and your mental well-being. Make the commitment to a better way of life. Eating organic food is more expensive, but it is a powerful way to voice change. If you buy organic and non-GMO food (GMO stands for Genetically Modified Organisms), you are voting through your food choices. If you buy non-organic or GMO food, you are supporting the continued supply of food that robs you of your aliveness. Don't let corporations cook for you!

Developing a love relationship with food is about making life-affirming food choices. You don't have to be perfect. Becoming more conscious about what you choose to eat will help you develop a love relationship with food.

Agri-business and what is happening with our food supply is a vast subject. I won't go into detail about how it has changed for the worse over the years. The main point is we have become disconnected from our food source. We shop at chain food stores and buy food that has traveled long distances to make it to the shelves. Often, we have no idea where the food came from or how it was processed. Food is now a big business (even organic food), and we are part of that big business. Even if we grow our own food, to some extent most of us still depend upon what is supplied to us and available in grocery stores. We need to reconnect with our food source and support that by purchasing healthy, life-giving foods.

Developing a love relationship with food is about making life-affirming food choices. You don't have to be perfect. Becoming more conscious about what you choose to eat will help you develop a love relationship with food.

We have all heard the saying, "You are what you eat." If you eat packaged and processed food, you will become more packaged and processed.

What I mean is further from your authentic self. If you eat real food, you will become more real. Therefore, choose food that is closer to its original state and its original source. For example, a locally grown organic apple from the farmer's market is closer to its original state and its original source than packaged apple slices from a supermarket. A head of organic broccoli from your local health food grocery store is closer to the source than a package of frozen broccoli.

When you eat, start to notice if the food is close to its original form. What type of packing did you have to open to eat or prepare it? Has it been changed or de-natured in any way? Is it still recognizable in its original form? I am not suggesting that all of your food must be in its original form. You will cook, cut and bake food. It will change in its form. However, be aware of how close your food is to its original source and how much food you take in that isn't.

Stop focusing on dieting, and start focusing on developing better, less obsessive eating habits. Dieting is not empowering! Throw out the idea of dieting. Every time you deny yourself something, you attract the opposite, indulgence. Under-eating leads to overeating. That's the way it works. Every time you under-eat, your body will want to overeat. Heal binge behavior by committing to never under-eat again. Denying yourself nutrition is a form of self-hatred. Care for yourself. Start listening to your body; start feeding it what it needs. Restricting yourself is abusive. If your body is craving something, then eat a moderate portion of it. Become aware of what your body needs...not what your mind likes. Real fresh food gives you the gift of vital life force energy to make you feel healthy, vibrant, alive and "thinking right." You will, over time, make healthier food choices naturally, not from a place of restriction or discipline, but from a place of choice.

Many wonderful foods will nourish and nurture your body. When you eat real food that nurtures and nourishes your body, you will get away from dieting and develop a closer relationship with your body. It will become easy to eat the right things. The best way to start feeding your body what it needs is to feed it non-packaged, non-processed, non-pesticide-sprayed food.

You may think you are eating healthy, but how much of your food comes from a package? How long has what you consume been in a warehouse before it gets to your stomach? What chemicals are in your food? How do they affect your mood, bodily functions, thoughts and intuitive connection with your body? How many sweets do you eat? Sugar brings the body out of balance. You don't have to eat white refined sugar to consume unhealthy sugar. Sugar includes glucose, fructose (fruit sugar), lactose (in milk), maltose (rice malt and honey), maple syrup, corn syrup and brown sugar. Alcoholic beverages are *loaded* with sugar. All these sugars, especially processed sugars, are to be consumed sparingly—if at all. Sugar feeds cancer and candida. If you want a sweet treat, eat a low-glycemic fruit, not a candy bar. Keeping your blood sugar levels balanced is important for optimal physical and emotional health.

The glycemic index is a measurement carried out on carbohydrate-containing foods and their impact on blood sugar. Eating high-glycemic foods increases your risk for developing diabetes and other health issues. Sugar and other high-glycemic foods wreak havoc on your body's equilibrium.

Our nation's disconnect from our food source directly relates to the disconnection we feel from our bodies and positive thought. Your food choices affect you. The more you eat closer to the source, fresh, natural, whole foods, the easier you will find it to love your body and get away from "artificial, packaged, processed thinking." *Wholesome eating leads to wholesome thoughts.* Eat a pear instead of canned pears. Eat cooked rice from bulk with fresh sautéed vegetables instead of a frozen rice and veggie dinner that proclaims "healthy" and "natural" on its packaging (even if it is from the health food store!). Because it is "normal" to eat fast food, packaged, and processed foods, we have lost our concept of what normal is. Your body can tell the difference! Your body, your temple, longs for "real" food. Start giving your body more "real" food, and your relationship with your body will transform. Don't do it only because you want your body to *look* good. Do it because you want to have a loving relationship with your body so it can *feel* good.

Make the commitment to spend your money, time, energy and effort on healthier, fresher food. Remember, doing so is an act of self-love. At times, you may be unable to eat as healthy as you would like. That happens at times, and it is okay to go with the flow. If you are eating less than healthy food, make sure you bless it. Better yet, bless all your food. Your food is sacred. Make it a habit to give thanks before you eat. Sometimes it is hard to remember, however if you make it a habit, it is a wonderful way to support your new love relationship with food.

HIGH VIBRATIONAL FOODS ARE SACRED

Food that is closer to its original source is a higher vibrational food. Higher vibrations release negative thought forms. The more our bodies get back to "real" food, the more we move toward health and the higher the vibration of our vital force. Remember, this is about being HAPPY. When you are happy, you are empowered. When unhappy or sad, you are not in your power or in a place of manifestation and creativity. You become stuck with low energy and lack of motivation. Negative thought forms are stored in the subtle system of the body at lower vibrational rates. When your body begins to vibrate at a higher level, the lower vibration thought forms that keep you stuck are forced out. They may come out in dreams, meditations, contemplation or just during the day. Eating high vibrational foods brings a release of old, limiting thought forms. Become aware of low-frequency food versus high-frequency food. Fresh, organic whole grains, fruit, vegetables and legumes are high-frequency foods. Processed, packaged, denatured and brutally slaughtered food sources are low frequency. Meat can be a high-frequency food if you acquire it from a humane, organic source.

In my younger years, I explored many diets. For a time in my life, I was a serious raw foodist. I was quite strict with my diet. Looking back, I realize my completely raw lifestyle was a way for me to isolate myself. As a raw foodist, I had a rigid lifestyle. I found peace with myself, my relationship with food, and other relationships when I opened myself to all healthy food.

The raw food lifestyle, unless I was with other raw foodists, meant sticking out in social situations. It meant not being able to eat this, or not being able to eat that, and always having some type of explanation as to why I couldn't eat or partake in a social situation fully. As a raw foodist, social gatherings were torturous for me. Eating and socializing are intertwined. I found that being 100 percent raw, even though I thought it would make me healthier, actually depleted me by keeping me from connecting with people I loved. I was playing an abusive restriction game with myself.

I would not recommend being completely raw. Being 60 to 80 percent raw is a good goal. Also, having cooked food brings in a level of warmth and nurturing that a raw diet doesn't offer. When I was a strict raw foodist, I was unconsciously trying to strip away all that was wrong with me. On an energetic level, I denied myself warmth and nourishment. Subconsciously, I had an attitude that everything in me needed to be cleansed and purified, instead of thinking I was perfect the way I was. Unknowingly, I was letting my diet be a way of self-rejection.

Raw food is still extremely healthy for you, especially raw organic food. I eat a lot of raw in my diet, especially during the summer. The difference is I do it from a place of choice, rather than *having* to. It is what my body wants, and I honor that. I am not white-knuckling it. It comes naturally, and is part of my life. Including lots of good raw organic food in your diet ensures you are bringing high-frequency nutrition into your body. Raw food that hasn't been denatured in any way emits a higher vibration.

Everything emits a vibration, because everything is energy. Every person emits energy. This energy is divine and permeates all of existence. Your energy field, or aura, is the energy you vibrate out into the world. It can be bright energy or dim energy. The same is true for food.

If you are tired or suffering from illness, your energy field is not as big as when you are healthy and feeling your best. This difference in energy fields has been scientifically measured using Kirlian photography. Kirlian photography is a photographic process that records electrical discharges naturally emanating from living objects, producing an aura-like glow or energy field surrounding the object. Packaged and processed food has had the life force energy beaten out of it, so to speak. What do you think your energy field would be like if you were tumbled down a conveyer belt, then poked, prodded, and filled with preservatives? You probably wouldn't feel energetically expanded.

A freshly picked apple just came from the powerful life-giving energy of the earth, where plants spring forth from the soil. That apple, if we were to take a Kirlian photograph of it, would be bright and shiny. Once the apple is picked and disconnected from the life-giving earth, the apple begins to lose its life force energy. A fresh-picked apple and a jar of applesauce may have similar nutrients. However, the life force energy the just-picked apple offers is far greater. Freshly harvested food provides nutrition and its life force energy. Fresh fruit and vegetables give us the gift of divine life force energy. We need this divine life force energy to feel optimistic, joyous and empowered.

Fruit signifies abundance. Though best eaten in moderation, fruit is part of a healthy balanced diet. Fruit enhances your vitality when eaten in moderation. Fruit is bright, vibrant and comes in beautiful colors. Fruit is from the flowering part of the plant. Fruit represents sweetness. Fruit is typically eaten raw and uncooked because it's naturally flavorful and perfect. Fruit is the best nutritional way to satisfy your desire for sweetness.

Vegetables help cleanse the body and release any darkness we are carrying emotionally, spiritually and physically. When you eat vegetables, you will feel brighter.

What has happened, though, is our desire for sweetness has become twisted. We are a culture addicted to sugar. I believe we are addicted to sugar because we have lost our sense of knowing we are sweet just the way we are. We want to fill ourselves up and not feel the pain. Is it possible that if you start experiencing the sweetness of who you are and the sweetness of life itself, that your sweet cravings will go away? It is a concept worth investigating. Do you consider yourself sweet? Do you treat yourself in a sweet way? If you suffer from sugar cravings, these questions are worth asking yourself.

Vegetables are also important for creating well-being in the body. Vegetables have vitamins, minerals and phytochemicals that create a healthy body and protect you from disease. Though vegetables come in different colors, many of them are green. This is because they contain chlorophyll. Chlorophyll is a pigment found in plants and is responsible for photosynthesis, a process that allows the plant to draw energy from light. The sun's rays shine on the plant, the plant draws energy from the sun, and it grows. In turn, you receive that light and energy from the plant when you eat it. Eating vegetables is a way to illuminate our bodies!

Vegetables help cleanse the body and release any darkness we are carrying emotionally, spiritually and physically. When you eat vegetables, you will feel brighter. Fresh, organic, unprocessed vegetables are one of the best antidepressants there are!

Chlorophyll also purifies our blood and has a rejuvenating effect on the body. Interestingly, chlorophyll's molecular structure is similar to that of blood. Hemoglobin is the substance in blood that carries oxygen from the lungs to the cells in the body. If you look at the structure of a molecule of *heme* (the portion of hemoglobin that carries oxygen) and a molecule of chlorophyll, you will see they are similar. The main difference is the heme molecule has iron in its center, and the chlorophyll molecule has magnesium in its center. There is something special happening here. Many of the components that build and sustain the essential elements in blood are found in foods that are high in chlorophyll. Your blood is the river of life that flows through you. Chlorophyll from vegetables is a way to illuminate your river of life and keep it flowing.

A beautiful relationship exists between respiration (the breath we take in and out) and the process of photosynthesis in plants. These two processes are interdependent and are essential to life on Earth. The inhalation of oxygen and expiration of carbon dioxide by all humans and animals complements the "inhalation" of carbon dioxide and expiration of oxygen by plants.

We are connected with the animal and plant world. They are our counterparts and companions. They are as much a part of us as we are a part of them. It is important to understand this sacred connection. They support us, and we need to support them if we are to live in harmony and experience the bounty of life springing forth on this planet. If we live in harmony with this process and acknowledge its power and gift, we can feel more alive and connected. We will experience the powerful source of energy moving through all things and moving through our bodies.

Vegetables, through their green chlorophyll, directly affect our hearts and illuminate us. They help our hearts shine brighter. The body has chakra systems, energy wheels in different areas along the body from top to bottom. Each chakra, or wheel of energy, represents different areas of development of our consciousness. Each chakra has a specific color and frequency. The heart chakra, located in the center of your chest, is the center for love. The consciousness it helps you develop is to love others and yourself. The color of the heart chakra is green. Colors affect our moods. The color green can help open our hearts.

Can eating more green leafy vegetables help you open your heart? David Wolf, author of *Longevity Now* and many nutrition books, said, "When you are green inside you are clean inside." Chlorophyll helps cleanse your blood and bring more oxygen into it. This opens the physical, emotional and energetic channels in your body that are clogged, resulting in you experiencing more of your expansive self.

Fruits and vegetables also contain phytochemicals, compounds that occur naturally in plants. Some create the deep colors such as those found in blackberries. Others create the strong smell such as those found in garlic. They have biological significance, and scientists estimate that as many as 10,000 different phytochemicals have a positive effect against disease in the body. Phytochemicals are magical helpers to keep us feeling bright, alive and illuminated.

Vitamins, especially from "real" food, are the givers of life. Vitamins have diverse biochemical functions. Some have hormone-like functions as regulators of mineral metabolism (such as vitamin D), or regulators of cell and tissue growth and differentiation (such as some forms of vitamin A). Others function as antioxidants, such as vitamin E and vitamin C. The largest number of vitamins, including the B complex vitamins, are precursors for enzyme cofactors. They help enzymes in their work as catalysts in metabolism. Enzymes are crucial to help break down the food you eat to harness the energy and life-giving force it offers.

Minerals are just as important to our health as vitamins. Like vitamins, minerals function as coenzymes, enabling the body to function. Minerals are essential for proper maintenance and well-being of our human body. Minerals are naturally occurring elements found in the earth and soil. The higher the content of minerals in the soil, the more nutritious the food that grows in it. "Real" food, as opposed to packaged and processed food, offers us more phytochemicals, vitamins and minerals to feel more empowered in our bodies.

Our bodies are made from minerals such as calcium and phosphorus. A mineral is an element or chemical compound that is normally crystalline in structure. The elements or chemical compounds carry information to our cells to create optimum health. Minerals can be found in many foods, including meat.

This brings me to the subject of eating meat. Meat eating is engrained in our culture. I am not here to say, "Eat meat" or "Don't eat meat." That is a personal decision. Eat what feels right for you and your body. However, I will say that as a culture, we eat more meat than we need, and it has a negative effect on our ability to stay healthy and feel our vitality. Also, the meat we eat is often not humanely handled and is pumped up with steroids and hormones.

If you are a meat eater, I suggest you eat less meat and more vegetables if you desire optimal health and want to feel alive in your body. Here is something to consider.

The biggest animals on the planet (bulls, elephants, rhinos and gorillas) are vegetarians. They grow to thousands of pounds with a diet consisting of twigs and leaves. They don't eat meat. If this is the case, then how much meat does a human need to eat to be strong and healthy?

I was a vegetarian for many years. I added a little meat to my diet when I found that having a dense protein helped balance my blood sugar. Still, I don't eat a lot of meat, and I make sure it is organic. I believe some people do better when they include a small amount of meat in their diets. I am one of those people. I am grateful to the animals that died so I can feel stronger in my body. It is a humbling feeling, and I don't take that gift lightly.

Changing to a healthier diet is a process; it ebbs and flows. Sometimes you eat healthier than you do at other times. Be gentle with yourself.

Though meat plays a role for many in their nutritional needs, vegetables are a key element for feeling alive and healthy. Overall, you probably don't consume enough whole, real, organic, unprocessed and unpackaged vegetables. Vegetables are a major guardian of our health and aliveness. Often when people want to eat healthier, they begin by adding more fresh fruit to their diets. Fruit is wonderful, don't get me wrong; however, if that's all you change, then fruit just adds more sugar to your diet. Focus on getting those magical daily greens into your diet. It will create a big difference in your overall health and happiness.

Changing to a healthier diet is a process; it ebbs and flows. Sometimes you eat healthier than you do at other times. Be gentle with yourself. You may be emotionally attached to certain foods. Stopping something cold turkey isn't always the best way to change a habit, unless an urgent health issue calls for immediate change.

If you are accustomed to having a big hamburger every week or a chocolate bar every day, then don't deprive yourself completely. Eating healthy and becoming more alive in your body is not about deprivation. It is about abundance. In other words, keep eating your beloved hamburger or cherished chocolate and start adding rich, juicy, wholesome organic vegetables to your diet. For the most part, keep eating the same way, but add raw or lightly steamed vegetables every day. If you take this type of attitude of adding to instead of taking away, you will begin to change your diet for the better. Don't focus on what you can't eat. Instead, focus on making sure you get your magical greens every day.

It takes 21 days to change a habit. You will crave more of whatever you eat. If you eat lots of starchy foods, you will crave starchy foods. If you eat salty foods, you will crave salty foods. If you consume a lot of sugar, your body is going to call out for and crave more sugar! The good news is that if you eat lots of vegetables, your body will start craving vegetables. It is a great feeling when you, naturally, without discipline, choose vegetables over less healthy foods.

When I was a raw foodist, I consumed lots of kale. One morning I woke up and found myself craving kale! Start eating more vegetables. Your body will love it and ask for more. The "bad" foods may not completely fall away, but over time, they will become less important. Your body will thank you for it.

I love vegetables, and am committed to eating them in their highest form as regularly as possible, along with other balanced components in my diet. Do I do that all the time? No. However, I make it a focus and for me, it is working. I don't beat myself up if I don't accomplish my vegetable goal every day. And I don't beat myself up for eating all the other things that aren't so good for me. I don't want to restrict myself regarding food. It only causes me to obsess more when I restrict my food. I highly recommend you adopt the same attitude.

Green Drink

One of the best ways to ensure you get your vegetables for the day is to make a green drink daily. My Vitamix® blender has been a great investment for my health. You can use another blender as long as it is a high quality, powerful blender. Juicing is also beneficial. I prefer blending my vegetables instead of juicing them because it takes less time and because blended vegetables, unlike juiced vegetables, maintain their fiber. Fiber will prevent constipation. Blending fruits and vegetables in my blender first thing in the morning for my breakfast helps me get my "quota" of greens for the day.

There are different ways to make a green drink. I make mine first thing in the morning, because if I don't, chances are I won't make it later in the day. Sometimes I make enough to have my breakfast green drink and then another glass of green drink later in the day. All I have to do is fill the Vitamix full instead of half full. This works out well, especially when I am on the go. If I leave the house and I am out all day, I know I will get hungry. I pack my green drink and some organic meat in an iced lunch bag and take it with me. Otherwise, I have a nice big green drink once a day.

There are different ways to make a green drink. I will give you an example. You can then vary it to fit your needs and your taste requirements. To make my green drink, I fill the Vitamix pitcher 1/3 with water, and then I add fruit and vegetables. I typically put in zucchini, cucumber, dandelion, avocado, lettuce, and a pear or apple. Sometimes I add spinach, celery or broccoli. I also add coconut oil and some herbs, such as powdered nettles and turmeric. Coconut oil has many health benefits such as regulating your metabolism and having anti-viral and anti-bacterial properties. The herb nettles is an overall health tonic; and turmeric is an anti-inflammatory. I blend this up, and then put half in a big glass. I put the other half in the refrigerator for later that day. Voila! I have gotten all of my vegetables, plus fiber, in for the day. The second green drink is a bonus. If you don't have a Vitamix, I recommend you make it a staple in your kitchen.

A blended green drink is fast, easy and tasty. It supports your health. It gives your digestive system a break since it is a liquid meal. It adds raw, high frequency vegetables and fruit to your diet. If you are not accustomed to the taste of green drinks, add more fruit to make it sweeter. As your taste buds get used to it, decrease the amount of fruits you use. I can't say enough about making a green drink part of your daily routine if you want to feel vibrant, empowered and healthy in your body.

Using the words "addiction" and "drug of choice" may be extreme, but I want to make a point. We use people, places and things—often unknowingly—to keep us from being present in our bodies and relationships. This prevents us from feeling empowered and fully vital in our bodies, lives and relationships.

FOOD: YOUR DRUG OF CHOICE

Changing your diet and making healthy food choices is a wise thing to do. But no matter how healthy your diet, if food is your drug to quell uncomfortable feelings, it will make your body out of balance. You will not be fully empowered in your body. Food obsession is a form of addictive behavior. I use the word "addiction" to underscore the severity of this issue.

Food addiction keeps you from your full potential. We all have a drug of choice to quell uncomfortable feelings. Life can be harsh with its daily challenges, and things can get uncomfortable without you realizing it. Turning to food can be a way to reward yourself, a way to make you feel good. Eating is a form of self-soothing. When done in balance, it can be a good thing. However, when the food you consume is out of balance, the result is food addiction.

Using the words "addiction" and "drug of choice" may be extreme, but I want to make a point. We use people, places and things—often unknowingly—to keep us from being present in our bodies and relationships. This prevents us from feeling empowered and fully vital in our bodies, lives and relationships.

According to the well-known psychology magazine, "Psychology Today," addiction is a condition that results when a person ingests a substance (e.g., alcohol, cocaine, nicotine, food) or engages in an activity (e.g., gambling, sex, shopping) that can be pleasurable, but the continued use/act ... becomes compulsive and interferes with ordinary life responsibilities.

Obsessive overeating, followed by self-induced vomiting, purging or fasting is known as *bulimia*, a medical/emotional disorder. It can become an addiction, even a life-threatening condition. At the other end of the spectrum, *anorexia nervosa*, causes people to obsess about their weight and the food they eat. They attempt to maintain a weight that is far below their normal range. This also can be a life-threatening condition.

Those caught in the grips of anorexia nervosa or bulimia build strong pathways in the brain, as discussed earlier, to support that habitual behavior. They have to go through a form of severe trauma to free themselves from these powerful diseases. They must go through a form of grief, similar to letting go of a good friend they have turned to for self-soothing and support. In food addictions and disorders, that friend—food—never talked back, was always there, and helped sooth life's misery.

We all have unique ways to deal with life and stress that robs us of our life force. Alcohol is common, such as when we have a drink to "take the edge off." Society supports, and joins us in, this behavior. Bars have "happy hours." In most populated areas of the country, you'll have no problem finding alcohol in grocery stores, restaurants, liquor stores or bars. Some turn to gambling, overworking, sex, shopping or even over-cleaning. Some of our "drugs," such as food and alcohol, are in the open and easily available. Others, such as sex, are not as public.

We turn to these behaviors to numb ourselves. We stop the flow of life force energy in our bodies because we don't want to feel an uncomfortable feeling. This happens all the time, every day. It becomes a way of life. We have learned to check out instead of check in. From this point of view, what do you use to numb yourself from the joys of life?

Women have other obsessions, but food is often a common "drug of choice" for us. Food is sensual; we are sensual. Food is nurturing; we are nurturers. Women often spend a lot of time in the kitchen preparing and cooking food. We are a perfect match with food. Do you turn to food to quell uncomfortable feelings? What age were you when it started? Our early programming with food creates a deep mark in our psyche.

CHILDHOOD PROGRAMMING

Food has always been my drug. Please understand I use the word "drug" here loosely as a term to describe anything we use to avoid being present, especially present with uncomfortable situations in our lives. The uncomfortable situation can be boredom, impatience, sadness, loneliness or any number of daily life experiences.

I would like to present the idea that, in a sense, we are *all* drug addicts, looking for some way to soften the tough existence we go through in the grind of life. I can use shopping and alcohol as my drug. But ultimately, food is where I end up. You may think using the word drug is harsh or extreme. My intention is for you to see how you may be missing the subtle pleasures of daily living associated with simply being present. Think about it. Do you have a "drug of choice" in your life? Does a certain behavior keep you from feeling the most alive that you can feel?

Life would be too painful if we didn't have these perceived pleasures to keep us, shall I say, preoccupied. We find peace in balance. I had to look at food, my drug of choice, and realize it had been a way for me to check out. It was a lifelong issue, and I wanted to find peace with it.

On the positive side, food and your relationship with it can be a compass for growth as you find balance and peace with it. If food is an issue for you, it is good to look at the source of this issue in your life. The behavior can develop very early in life, for some even as infants. For me, emotional eating started when I reached puberty. Two strong circumstances led me to use food as my "drug": family dinners during childhood, and gymnastics competition.

I remember having to do the dishes after dinner. I was the middle child, one of five children. I had an older brother, an older sister and two younger sisters. My mother always left the girls in charge of doing the dishes after dinner. I was a rebel and didn't understand why my brother didn't have to do the dishes, too. My mother said he did the gardening and pulled weeds, but he didn't have to do that every day, or at least I didn't see him out there pulling weeds every day. I love my brother, and we've even talked about this in our adult life. He is a wonderful father, who has since done plenty of dishes while raising his own children. I wasn't against him. I was against the "injustice" we girls endured. Since we all ate, I thought we all should help in the cleanup. I felt angry and needed to be heard and understood.

As I took my turn in the kitchen to do the dishes, I ate the leftovers instead of putting them into little containers and into the refrigerator. I could never find the right-size container or the matching lid. In my frustration, and realizing there wasn't much food worth saving anyway,

I ate it. The rebel in me was upset because the idea of my brother taking his turn in the kitchen wasn't supported. Eating the leftovers, though at that time unconscious to me, helped me quell and disconnect myself from the uncomfortable feelings of anger, sadness and even fear that I was experiencing. My stomach was already satisfied after having eaten dinner. By the time I was done with the dishes, I was uncomfortably full.

At the same age, the second biggest influence in making food my drug of choice and developing body-image issues fit hand in glove with the dinner dishes issue. I started dieting to lose weight for my gymnastics coach. He was a young, handsome man in charge of ten or eleven young girls. He had a private gymnastics club. When we practiced, we wore tight gymnastic suits that just covered our torsos. Our legs, which were still little-girl legs, but quickly flowering into beautiful women's legs, were completely exposed.

My parents had good intentions, and on many levels, gymnastics was an empowering experience and good for me. On other levels, it was the beginning of my roller-coaster ride with food and of developing a distorted view of my body.

If you look at the picture of me with my teammates, you will see I am the tall one (See fig. 11.1). The other girls were petite and much shorter. I was thin and tall, and compared to the girls on the team, I felt *big*. To be a great gymnast, it is best to be tiny and fit. I was fit, but I wasn't tiny, height-wise. At that time, I was probably 5' 5". I am now 5' 7" and love being tall. For gymnastics, though, most of the girls were tiny and short.

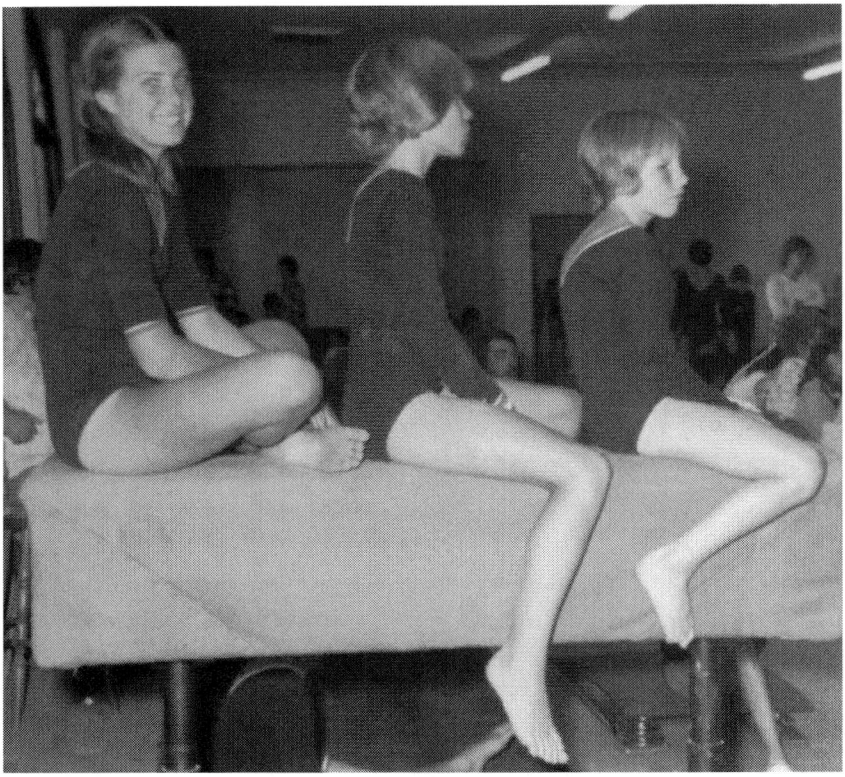

Figure 11.1

Here I am with my younger sister and another gymnastics teammate. I was not fat however as you can see, I was much bigger than the other girls on the team. This did not help the false perspective I was developing at a young age about my body.

I was athletic as a child, and tumbling got me interested in gymnastics. On some levels, I was a misfit on the team. I couldn't do the parallel bars well because it took a tremendous amount of arm strength, which I didn't have to match my long, tall body. The shorter girls could whip around those parallel bars in nothing flat. Vaulting always scared me. It seemed so violent. The balance beam was fun, because I could focus on balance and form, but I did best in floor exercise. I couldn't do all the acrobatic tricks, but I was graceful. I believe I was the most graceful girl on the team. The other girls could do the acrobatic tricks, but I could move my body in a beautiful and flowing way. I remember that. My arms were long, and my fingers were graceful as they flowed through the air as I executed the floor routine. For me, that was fun. It was an opportunity for me to connect with the feminine, sensual woman I was becoming.

When I think back, I believe that the feminine, sensual woman budding inside of me wasn't fully safe at those gymnastic workouts because my gymnastic coach always wanted me to lose a few pounds. I wasn't fat. I was always a skinny kid, but I was flowering, coming into womanhood at the vulnerable age of 14. That was the age when I started my cycle.

There I was, half-clothed with my teammates, standing in front of a young man as he showed us the ins and outs of gymnastics, spotted us and touched our bodies as we practiced gymnastic moves and routines. There was nothing malicious about my coach. He was a fine man and did a great job creating his own company and private gymnastics team. My parents supported me as I trained in an area that interested me – a sport that included elements of acrobatic performance, art and dance. I loved it and was dedicated to gymnastics. On the downside, gymnastics was competitive, grueling and un-nurturing to my vulnerable female body that was flowering. I didn't want to accept the idea that one person was better than another. Competitive sports encourage that. Nonetheless, gymnastics gave me a platform in which I could move my body and express myself in a graceful way.

My gymnastics coach, as I said, wanted me to lose a few pounds to increase my performance. I was young and didn't know anything about dieting or losing weight. He recommended that I start eating protein. He said a high protein diet would make me lose weight. Knowing nothing about dieting, and having received only the instruction to eat protein, I began to eat lots of nuts and peanut butter on lettuce. I had no idea how to go about this protein diet, and ended up putting on a few pounds. The more I focused on what to eat and what not to eat, and the more I obsessed about food, the more weight I gained. It was the beginning of the insanity in my relationship with food and my body.

I didn't gain lots of weight while I was on the gymnastics team, but I did begin the crazy-making lifestyle of dieting and hating my body. I don't think I was ever meant to carry a lot of extra body weight. My body is too sensitive, my mind too active and my desire to move my body regularly is too strong for me to become heavy set. I am an active person, and I mean physically active. An ex-boyfriend once told me I couldn't do enough exercise to calm my mind. When he said that, I knew there was some validity in his statement. I need to move my body in some form on a regular basis in order to calm my mind and feel sane in this world. I have had to do that all my life. It has been a good thing. It has kept me fit. I was a fanatic about exercise in my earlier years. I now have a more balanced approach to exercise.

One day at gymnastics practice, I felt lightheaded. I knew something wasn't quite right. I was diagnosed with an acute case of mononucleosis. I had to stay home for weeks and get home schooling for a while because I was so sick. I recovered, but I lost quite a bit of weight. When I returned to gymnastics, I was happy because I knew I had lost weight. I thought the coach would notice and be pleased. He only said that I could lose a few more pounds. I was hurt and disappointed, though at the time I didn't process my feelings.

What a devastating blow that was for an innocent girl. I had gotten sick; that's what it took to lose the weight he wanted me to lose. But still, it wasn't enough. Nothing was enough. This only added to the distorted self-image I was forming at that young, vulnerable age.

These two experiences in childhood, having to do the dishes (and battle for equal rights for women) and being half naked and not skinny enough for my gymnastics coach, were two circumstances that helped shape me into an all-American girl with food and body image issues.

What were your circumstances as a little girl as you developed into a woman? I am sure other circumstances also affected me, but the two I shared with you stand out. I said all-American girl because this problem of food issues and body image issues is common in our culture. It is nothing to be ashamed of. It is part of the great American way of life that we are here to heal. We will do that by overcoming it and seeing it for what it really is: a distorted perception of who we are as women. Once we realize what we are up against, we can begin the healing process.

We are all learning to become more conscious and empowered. Growing up, we experienced subconscious feelings based on external events. We live in an unconscious world, or a world that is in the process of becoming conscious. We are growing up together. It is a process. Each of us has experiences, stories and wounds to heal from as part of reclaiming our bodies and our full potential. It is important not to stay stuck in the stories or wounds from the past. Rather, use these as a way to develop compassion for yourself.

What wounding experiences gave you the fertilizing ground to develop your "drug of choice"? What childhood experiences did you have to make you want to numb out? There is no one to hate, and no one to blame for these experiences. Some of you had horrendous and unthinkable childhood experiences. My heart goes out to you. This is where forgiveness comes in. Hating those who harmed you will only rob you of your power.

Our parents, caregivers and mentors are only conscious and aware as far as society has developed. Today, parents have access to information and resources not available even twenty years ago. Babies, toddlers, children and teens have a tremendous number of needs. It is inevitable that at some point, their caregivers will fall short. They don't do it maliciously. They are doing the best they can with what they have and what they know.

I don't have children, except for one, my inner child. I have spent my adult life raising her so I don't repeat the non-affirming generational behavioral patterns that were passed down to me. My inner child has many needs and keeps me busy. You have an inner child, too. Have you ever connected with her?

Let me get back to the drug I chose to numb my uncomfortable feelings. I spent many of my younger years suffering and battling with food and my body. I even majored in dietetics as a way to find peace. I sold to health food stores after I graduated from college, and learned more about nutrition and healthy eating. The more I learned, the more I became a health nut. But always lingering in the background was my struggle with food obsession and body image.

All through my late teens, twenties and thirties I struggled with body image issues and food obsessions. I was a productive person and accomplished a lot. However, I also abused my body with overeating, followed by under-eating, or overeating, then over-exercising. I would diet and beat myself up. Beating myself up was the worst part. Hating myself and telling myself I shouldn't have eaten this or that, how big my stomach was, how horrible I felt, and how I couldn't keep doing this. I went to the gym to burn off calories for what I had eaten. If I ate too much one day, I carried a dark cloud around in my consciousness the next day. It was heavy energy and a dark secret of mine for many years. I suffered alone. I didn't seek help. I was ashamed to share openly with those close to me that I'd had too much to eat the day before. I could share that about alcohol, but with food, I was too ashamed to say I had overeaten. It was a burden to carry this secret. It went on for many years, inner turmoil and what I consider abusive inner dialogue. I wanted this obsession to go away. The more I wanted it to go away, the more it stayed. I didn't want it in my life. I hated it! I wanted to have a normal relationship with food, like everyone else did. I had no idea others were suffering the similair depths of pain. And though I suffered, I could convince myself it wasn't that bad.

When I began to understand that we all have addictions or not-so-healthy ways to quell our uncomfortable feelings, I began to feel a change. What you do to quell uncomfortable feelings is unique to you. It doesn't go away. It is uniquely part of you and it is yours for life. I came to understand that I was programmed from childhood to use food to quell my uncomfortable feelings, and that this wasn't going to go away. What I actually needed to do was accept it as part of me. That was the turning point for me, and the beginning of my healing process with food and body image issues.

I began to find peace when I understood that I obsessed about food and my body because I wanted to quell uncomfortable feelings. I learned not to shame myself for it afterwards. I began to accept that I am an emotional eater. I tried it on for size. I acknowledged it. I accepted that it wasn't going to go away anytime soon, and that it was a part of me. Once I committed to noticing when I would beat myself up and shifting that, it was the beginning of creating a more harmonious relationship with food and my body.

If you are an emotional eater and would like to heal, know that you are not alone. Others are suffering, just like you. Know that no matter how hard you try not to be an emotional eater, you will always be one. Fully accepting that you are an emotional eater is pivotal to healing it. Can you admit you use food to quell uncomfortable emotions? Can you accept and love yourself when you are uncomfortably full or have a food hangover from the day before? Can you commit to never beating yourself up with inner dialogue that is abusive because you ate either too much or something you were "not supposed to eat"? Can you instead commit to being your cheerleader? Let go of self-criticism and commit to being gentle and compassionate with yourself in these situations.

DANCING ~~INSTEAD OF~~ EATING

Another big turning point for me occurred one magical evening after I'd been out on a date. I was able to be there for myself and quell my uncomfortable feelings instead of turning to food and binging.

I believe, especially for women, non-food related, healthy, wholesome sensual pleasure is the antidote to body image issues and overeating. I experienced this when I went on the first date after my husband died. I was thirty-nine when he passed away. We were together for eleven years. He was a wonderful man, and I loved him beyond words. About a year after he passed away, I was with my girlfriend at the Voo-Doo Lounge at the top of the Rio Hotel in Las Vegas, where I lived at the time. A handsome man took interest in me, and we started to chat. He was vacationing from out of town. He asked me out for dinner and a show the following evening. I accepted the invitation. I was excited about the date, and got dressed up in a sexy outfit for the evening.

I hadn't been single for more than eleven years. The last time I was single, I was much younger, so this was a new experience for me. I met my date at the casino, and he took me to dinner. I remember having a cocktail and feeling as though I was being treated like a queen. After dinner, we went to a show. After the show, he walked me to my car and we said our good-byes. He didn't ask me out on another date, and he didn't even try to kiss me or make other sexual advances. The last time I was single and dating, my experience was that sexual advances were standard.

My date that night was a perfect gentleman. Maybe he was married, and keeping that a secret, or maybe he wasn't interested. Who knows? All I know is that as I drove home, I began to feel a strong craving to eat, to have something sweet, to fill my belly. I'd already had a nice dinner, and I was certainly not hungry. I was having an uncomfortable feeling. My usual behavior was to numb it with food, often without even noticing that I was having an uncomfortable feeling.

I remember getting the craving on the freeway on my way home. There was a 24-hour coffee shop right off the freeway, a couple of exits before mine. When I was a mile or so from the exit, I thought about getting off the freeway, going into the coffee shop, and ordering a nice big plate of pancakes with lots of butter and syrup. I imagined how delicious those pancakes would taste and what a pleasurable experience the first bite would be. I began to get excited thinking about those pancakes.

This desire for food was not uncommon for me. I had a love/hate relationship with food. When these cravings came for me, the effort to push away the overwhelming desire was so strong that I could never control these urges. I always ended up eating more than I should, feeling guilty about it and feeling physically out of balance afterwards. This time was different because I was able to connect to my vulnerable little girl inside. As I approached the exit, I began to talk to myself. I took one hand off the steering wheel, held my belly and talked to myself in a nurturing, compassionate and even parental way. I realized I was having sweet cravings due to how the date ended. I wondered if I was desirable.

I told the deepest most vulnerable part of myself, "Honey, you are beautiful. Just because he didn't try to kiss you or make sexual advances, doesn't mean you are not sexy. You are beautiful, sexy and wonderful. You don't need a man to tell you that. I am telling you that right here and right now, and I want you to know it. You don't need those pancakes. They won't get you where you want to go. They won't make you feel good. You know that if you go and have pancakes, then you are just going to go home and raid the refrigerator, and that won't be good for you either. Let's just go home and dance. I want to take you home and we can dance together, just you and me." At that point, I mustered up the courage, focus, or whatever it took, to pass the exit to the 24-hour coffee shop. Instead, I drove myself home.

When I got home, I turned on some sensuous music, put a chair in the middle of the living room and began to dance for *myself.* My living room had big windows that, in the night, were like mirrors. I used the chair as a prop, and watched myself as I danced sensuously, erotically and beautifully to the music. It felt so good to move my body to the music and feel my sensual feminine nature oozing out of me with every move. I engaged fully in those moments of sensual expression, enjoying it to the fullest degree. As that ecstatic experience ended, I felt peaceful, centered and balanced. For the very first time in my life, I had taken myself down a different road than I had always taken in the past. Instead of succumbing to my desire to numb the uncomfortable feeling by overeating, I danced. I felt as if I had found my way home.

This was a transformational experience for me. It was the first time I was able to be there for that little girl inside who wanted to feel loved and accepted. I made contact with her. I was there for her, and my wise woman was able to guide her in a better direction. What a powerful experience it was for me. Prior to that night, the only way my cravings would go away was to succumb to them and feed my face. I hated that about myself. I had been through it so many times before. Nothing could ever stop me. That night, dancing sensually for myself did.

Putting my hand on my belly, being there for myself, encouraging myself, choosing a sensual pleasure that was life enhancing instead of life robbing was what I needed more than I needed pancakes. It was so empowering to know I could shift my undesirable behavior. I felt free!

There are many sensual and soul-freeing activities you can do instead of turning to food. Emotional eating is simply a habit that can be changed. Here are some things you can do to create a more sensual, sane and empowered life, one that supports your sensual, feminine essence.

10 THINGS TO DO
INSTEAD OF EMOTIONAL EATING

1. Take a bath.
2. Take a walk.
3. Dance sensually.
4. Belly breathe.
5. Cry and hold yourself.
6. Do a guided meditation.
7. *Stop* and ask yourself, "What do I need right now?"
8. Feel the desire, and see what is underneath it.
9. Sensually pleasure yourself.
10. Clean your house.

EXERCISE:

Make your own list of ten things you can do instead of emotional eating. Write it here, and then make a copy. Put it on your refrigerator, in your refrigerator, on your bathroom mirror or wherever you feel it will be most effective.

1. Dance.
2. Yoga
3. Meditate
4. Revise alt. methods of nurturing self
5. Streamline energy into diff. tasks
6. Wonder why.
7. Apply favourite scent.
8. Feed my mind
9. Walk.
10. Deep breaths.

CHAPTER 4

Having A Love Affair With Your Body

Your body is yours
If you listen to her, she will open many doors

Doors of love, elation and sensual delight
Enjoying how it feels oh so right

Listen to your body and she will give you many things
Tune into her and see how beautifully she sings

In the previous chapter, we discussed how to empower yourself by enhancing the type of relationship you have with food. We talked about sensuality being a part of your nature as a woman. We discussed identifying ways to satisfy your innate sensuality through wholesome, life-enhancing sensual experiences as opposed to life-robbing behaviors. In this chapter, we will discuss the importance of deepening your relationship with your body and empowering yourself by creating a love affair with it.

BODY IMAGE

Your body is your temple, though most of us treat our bodies like we treat a rental car. With all the stimuli we are exposed to in the media and in society, most women have adopted an "if only" perspective about their bodies. *If only my hips were smaller, if only my breasts were larger, if only my smile were straight, if only my legs were thinner, if only my legs were thicker.* This is living in your head about your body. If judgment is the only type of relationship you have with your body, it becomes an abusive existence.

Having a love affair with your body changes this abusive existence into a life that is nurturing, loving and supportive. I mentioned earlier that pleasure is the antidote to food and body image issues. You accomplish this by establishing a more sensual, instead of mental, relationship with your body.

A woman's body is sensual, and women are innately sensual beings. Our culture has not given us a safe place to be sensual. Our sensuality has been bottled up with a price tag on it. It is often only expressed in less than nurturing places for women, such as strip clubs. I am not against strip clubs. It just seems that most of them don't provide an environment that supports a loving and nurturing way of life for women.

We live in an anti-ecstatic world. Women, as sensual beings, have had to wall off or compartmentalize that part of them to survive in this world. With that compartmentalizing and walling off, lots of negative symptoms develop because we are swimming upstream and away from that which we naturally are. We develop an unhealthy need for approval and express our sensuality as a way to entice or control. We pretty ourselves up to appeal to the opposite sex instead of simply wanting to express and exude the delightful feminine essence we inherently hold within us. Often we go to great lengths, striving to conform to the ideal of what society depicts as beautiful.

Have you spent lots of time and energy trying to make your body something that it is not? If you have short legs, have you longed for them to be longer? If you have curly hair, do you blow it straight? Do you wish for a flatter stomach or thinner legs?

For years, I wanted to have a gap between my thighs. I tried so hard, with dieting and exercise, to make my legs skinnier. No matter how hard I tried, I couldn't diet or exercise my way into that darn gap between my thighs like the models had. Even after a bout with appendicitis, where I lost a lot of weight, my legs still touched at the top! I had to learn to love my legs the way they were. They weren't going to have that desired gap or space that models have. It wasn't going to happen, no matter how hard I tried.

The wild part is that my legs are beautiful. For years, I just wanted them to be perfect or even thinner. People often commented on how nice and long my legs are, but I never appreciated them. Now I do. I have learned to love them just the way they are. Recently, I listened to my legs during a guided body meditation, and I learned to love them even more. The meditation was specifically designed to take us through our bodies and make a connection with them. It was designed for us to learn to honor and listen to our bodies.

When it came to my legs, I was guided to listen to what my legs had to say. They told me they didn't want to be separate from each other. They wanted to touch at the top and be connected! I had already worked through many of my body image issues years before, and had established a deep love for my body, but this extra message from my legs was like having the cherry on top. It was a beautiful message from my legs that they liked being together and didn't want to be separate. I loved it!

What parts of your body do you wish were different? Energetically, when you dislike a body part, you cut off energy in that area. You disempower a part of yourself. You create a battle between your mind and that part of your body. That area of your body then lives in a contracted state, which means that part of your body is cut off from your aliveness, sensuality and ability to feel pleasure. The benefit of stopping such an internal battle with yourself is you will start feeling more sensually alive. You will start feeling more empowered in your body, your femininity and your sexuality. In order to achieve this full empowerment, you need to have positive regard for *every* part of your body, especially those parts of your body that you "think" are not so perfect.

Accepting your perceived imperfections is a major step towards your empowerment as a woman.

Accepting your perceived imperfections is a major step towards your empowerment as a woman. You will start to experience your body as your sacred temple. Start paying attention to the words you say about your body or body parts. Are they kind; are they loving; are they critical? What happens when someone criticizes you? Don't you contract? How about when someone appreciates you and says kind things to you? Don't you feel more expanded and alive? The same thing happens with you and your relationship with your body. The cells in your body will respond to your positive words. On a cellular, energetic level, your body will become more alive and empowered. You will develop a sense of positive regard for your body.

In order to have an empowering relationship with your body, you need to understand it, listen to it and illuminate it. Hold your body, and your thoughts about it, in the highest regard; have a love affair with your body. These actions are life affirming and enlivening. Let's begin with the concept of understanding your body.

UNDERSTANDING YOUR BODY

Understanding your body will help you hold it in high regard. I am not referring to understanding your body as a medical doctor would. You don't need a medical degree, or any degree, to understand your body. Of course, education about your body is good and can support you in understanding your body on a deeper level. However, I am referring to understanding your body by tuning into it. You want to create a relationship with your body, from the inside out. This can be a lifelong process.

The more you bring in the frequency of love into your life experiences, the more you can shine the unlimited and powerful source of universal light through your body.

Your body is an amazing work of art. It is created from crystalized fields of thought manifested from your level of consciousness. Matter consists of light and that light is always changing and evolving. Your soul is light and the source of all creation is light. You hold the source of creation within you. It becomes manifest through your thought-forms. Your body is your suit through which you travel your journey of life and express this light. Your body is a crystallization of your consciousness into form.

Your life experiences are an outer expression of your inner dialogue that is created from this crystallized consciousness. Your light is the storehouse of your mind and your mind creates your unique world. The more you bring in the frequency of love into your life experiences, the more you can shine the unlimited and powerful source of universal light through your body.

No matter what your spiritual orientation, you probably would agree that our bodies are both spiritual and physical. The physical part is the animal part. Your body is the animal part of you, and therefore your body is your closest pet. You might treat your cat or dog better than you treat your body. Realize that your body is your closest pet, and start to care for it as you would a pet that you love dearly so that your light can shine.

Understand that your body needs kind words in order to shine brightly. Understand that your body needs your acceptance in order to shine brightly. Understand that your body needs to feel appreciated in order to shine brightly. Enhancing your relationship with it and understanding its needs are crucial to your empowerment as a woman. You personify leading from a place of love when you deeply love your body. You open yourself up to the creative power of the universe.

What would your life be like if you could accept your body in all of its uniqueness? This means accepting your body as it is right now, this very moment, this very day. Not ten pounds lighter or some other body in the future. Love the body you have right now. If your stomach sticks out a bit, then love that extra bulge. Be kind to it. Don't abuse it with negative mind chatter. Your body has feelings, actually many feelings. The more you talk negatively about or to your body, the more your body will contract and become less powerful, and the less your powerful and radiant feminine light will shine.

I remember once, during my obsessive years, feeling fat from overeating. The next day, I felt horrible in my body. I looked into the mirror, stared at my body and felt anxiety because I had put on a bit of weight. I was fear-stricken, and I felt it in every cell. I felt the lack of acceptance in every cell in my body. I felt the discomfort of not wanting to be in my body and not wanting to be myself in that moment. It was a horrible, disempowering experience, all driven by negative thoughts.

Feminine energy is soft and nurturing, and your body needs that. Through my negative self-image, I was destroying my connection to my body. I wasn't letting myself be who I was in that moment, and my body responded with disgust in every cell. Have you ever not wanted to be in your body? Have you ever felt disgust in every cell?

> ***True feminine power is about feeling more, not weighing less.***

Your body was designed for pleasure. You have erogenous zones all over your body. Erogenous zones are areas on the body that have heightened sexual sensitivity. When your body responds to this less physical, more subtle energy, it will connect you to your divine feminine power. You will no longer treat your body with disgust when you honor your body's ability to experience heightened sensitivity. Heightened sensitivity also means that you are vulnerable to harshness. When something is sensitive, it can't handle harshness or something that isn't sensitive. A woman's body is sensitive, especially when it comes to the harsh words we tell it.

Start to pay attention to the words you say to your body. Are they kind? Are you often critical in your inner dialogue about your body? When you try on clothes at a store, are you critical of how the clothes fit? Do you wish you had a different body type? When you take a shower, how do you shower? Do you handle your body gently? Do you wash your genitals with adoring care? After showering, when you dry off, do you handle your body attentively and kindly? Your body is listening, and she is sensitive. Be sweet to her.

You cannot be sweet to your body if you obsess about your weight. If you are going to beat yourself up about the number on your scale, then throw away your scale. Weighing yourself every day with that type of attitude is abusive and will disconnect you from the beauty of who you are and how magnificent your body is. True feminine power is about feeling more, not weighing less.

Since we are innately sensual creatures, we have a strong desire to feel good in our bodies. If we do anything that doesn't nurture this, we obstruct our efforts to develop a deeper understanding of ourselves. We cut ourselves off from our inherent nature as women and disconnect from our body's wisdom. If you are harsh to your body, then you cut off your ability to hear everything it wants to tell you. Your body is both wise and powerful.

Understand that as a woman, you are an emotional, feeling, sensitive, sensual and complex person. You need a lot of love and reassurance. Be hyper vigilant about your needs and your body's needs. Bear in mind that we live in a masculine-oriented world. That means we are surrounded by a lot of masculine qualities expressed in our daily lives. Masculine qualities include being focused and driven, with a "get it done" type of energy. Masculine qualities also include being logical, rational and assertive. This is good, and it's important to balance the masculine with feminine qualities such as being receptive, nurturing, allowing and intuitive. In end effect, the masculine is steady, stable and strong; the feminine is flexible, fluid and flowing.

The masculine is steady, stable and strong; the feminine is flexible, fluid and flowing.

You may have seen the illustration depicting an operating switch for a man and one for a woman. The operating box for the man has a simple on and off switch. The operating switch for the woman contains various switches, dials, valves and regulators. The old paradigm was built from an on or off point of view, giving no space for anything in between. Women are complex. We are different from moment to moment. Some days are better than others. Some hours of the day are busier than others. We don't live in an on or off body... we live in a body that flows and constantly moves and changes.

I am not saying that men are not complex. Men have challenges and specific needs as well. We all have masculine and feminine energies in us. As all of us awaken our compassionate, intuitive, more receptive side, we will find harmony, especially with the opposite sex. This will create a better world. Since a woman's body holds the feminine, it is up to us to lead the way. We are leaders of the softer, intuitive, more receptive energies. That doesn't mean we have less power. Our power comes from those energies. Cultivating those energies begins with applying them to the relationship we have with our bodies.

Another important concept to understand is that your body responds to appreciation. The same way your body contracts when criticized, the opposite holds true: your body expands with positive self-talk and appreciation. Everyone wants to feel appreciated. Whether you receive or give appreciation, you will find it lifts the spirits of both the giver and the receiver. In the case of you appreciating your body, you receive and give appreciation. Giving appreciation shows that you value your body, and your body wants to be valued. We all want to be valued. Your body does many things for you. It digests your food, walks and takes you places, works for you and much more. It does many things that we take for granted. You get things done by using your body. The point is that your body needs appreciation for all it does for you.

Appreciation is also a form of recognizing and seeing the good. When you recognize someone, you remember that person from some time in the past. Recognizing your body, giving it recognition, is remembering. You already know that you have a beautiful, magnificent body. The knowing is already there, and all you have to do is remember it.

Worship is a deeper form of appreciation and recognition. A woman's body responds greatly to being worshipped. The word worship, in context with your body, may challenge your belief systems, or it may not. If it does, let me use some other words to describe what I mean, words that a woman's body responds to. Your body loves to be adored. It loves to be honored and treated in high regard. It loves to be recognized as sacred. If you want an intimate partner to worship your body, you need to worship it first. Cultivate a sacred relationship with your body.

The sacrum, a bone at the base of the spine, is where we hold our femininity. Sacrum, in Latin, means *sacred.* You are sacred, and your body is sacred. The sacrum (sacred bone) holds the blueprint of our human potential. Our blueprint, or Kundalini energy, is seated at the base of our spines, in the area of the sacrum. As we evolve and awaken to our full potential, this life force energy moves up the spine and we live more consciously.

Understand that your body is your temple. When people worship, where do they worship? They worship in churches or temples. Since your body is your temple, worshiping it is appropriate. Worshipping it will assist you in evolving to a greater level of awareness. The body's structure is, in part, created by the skeletal system. The bones of the skeletal system protect organs, support the body and allow us to be mobile. They produce red and white blood cells in the marrow portion of the bone. They also store minerals essential to life. The bone is mainly made up of a mineral called calcium phosphate. Minerals are crystals of light. Therefore, I like to refer to the body, due to its skeletal system, as a crystal temple of light made of calcium. Take a moment and feel into your skeletal system throughout your body. It is a crystal structure of light. Imagine that!

Barbara Brennan is a healer and teacher, and the author of *Hands of Light*. She founded Barbara Brennan School of Healing (BBSH), a school dedicated to the evolution of the human spirit. One paragraph in *Hands of Light* really hit home for me. I highlighted it when I first read it, and I have shared it with my students throughout the years. Here is what Barbara Brennan says about our bodies:

> *You have designed your body and your energy system as a tool to perform your life task. It is made up of a combination of energy consciousness that best suits what you have been incarnated to do. No one else has that combination and no one else wants to do precisely what you want to do. You are unique. When you block the flow of energy in your energy system that you created for your task, you also block your task. The general patterns of blocking that people do are called structures and defense systems. These are all ways by which you habitually separate yourself from what you came to do on the world task level. They are also direct manifestations of what you don't know about life that you have come here to learn. Therefore, you have your lesson crystallized into your body and your energy system. You have built and fashioned your schoolroom according to your own specifications. You live inside it!*

Understand that you designed your body. It is exactly what you want and need in order to complete your life task, what you came here to accomplish. You might think your body isn't perfect, but it is perfect for you, so don't criticize it. You chose to have the shape you have. There is no room to beat yourself up and think your body should be different. It is perfect for you, and you need it exactly the shape and size it is in order to live the life and learn the lessons your soul has planned for you.

Understanding that you designed your body can help you have a deeper acceptance of its unique shape and size. Knowing this can heal body image issues, because you realize that hating a certain shape or size of a body part is due to cultural conditioning rather than what your soul really wants.

The other point Barbara Brennan makes is that your body is specifically designed so you can accomplish your soul's purpose. Your soul's purpose is unique to you. No one else has the unique task you came to accomplish. If you block the energy flowing through your body (your uniquely designed temple), then you block your ability to complete what you came to do in this lifetime. For this reason, it's important to appreciate your body and keep her feeling alive and filled with vitality. Doing so will keep you connected to your soul's purpose, empower you and let you lead your life with love.

Brennan also points out that habitual patterns keep us from allowing our energy to flow freely and express our full potential. We don't learn in school how to take care of our physical, emotional and spiritual well-being. Reading, writing and arithmetic take precedence over such things. If we didn't learn how to take care of our well-being from our parents or our caregivers while growing up, then we have to learn it on our own. Instead, most of us learned to use our bodies as cheap rental cars that we can bang around and discard when we are done with them. With the all-American lifestyle, our bodies get quite banged up in a lifetime.

We all experience challenges in life. It is part of the journey, and part of our souls' maturation. If you let these challenges get you down instead of learning from them and creating greater awareness, you will begin to lose your life force energy. You will block yourself from the source of divine essence that will support you to complete your life task. If you are eating a SAD diet (Standard American Diet) in its denatured and lifeless form, you may not have the energy to stay motivated to even find out what your soul's purpose is.

The fascinating part is that the habitual repressing of uncomfortable feelings with unproductive behaviors separates you from what you came here to do. This is exactly the area where you lack awareness. They are the things you need to learn about life. What habitual patterns have held you back and kept you from your full potential? Your challenges are actually gifts. If you run from your challenges, you run from your aliveness. If you choose not to face your challenges, then you will harden as you grow older. Life isn't always easy. Life can get all of us down at certain points. You need tools like the "4 N's," the process I discussed earlier of Notice, Name, Nurture and Need. This tool and others I teach will show you how to express yourself from your heart instead of your head. They are tools that allow you to move towards greater understanding, forgiveness and compassion. These qualities will keep you feeling young, vibrant and empowered.

As the chakras open, our bodies open, our consciousness opens and we become more connected to the infinite power of the universe. The universe becomes part of our being, and we then live open-heartedly and feel more empowered in our bodies. The universal force fuels us; we are no longer fueled by our fears. Divine inspiration leads us instead of crippling depression. We have angels on our side instead of anger in our hearts.

The challenge in this body is to age gracefully. Tools help, and the rest is fate or destiny. Face the challenges of life and let them be a source of growth. When you allow yourself to face each challenge, and the people involved in those challenges, with an open heart, you are on the path to learning and accomplishing what you came here to do.

THE CHAKRA SYSTEM

Your body is beautifully and magically designed. It is the perfect vehicle in which to evolve your soul. Doing so requires letting divine light flow through it. Your soul wants to shine brightly from within your body. The chakra system part of yogic teachings consists of energy wheels located up and down the length of the body. These energy wheels, or chakras regulate the flow of light through your body. They hold different levels of consciousness from which your soul can shine out.

Chakra, translated from Sanskrit, means *wheel.* The body contains seven chakras, or wheels of light. Each wheel holds a specific level of awareness that supports your soul's maturation and illumination. The chakras are designed to help us learn the lessons we need to learn to live a fully empowered life. As the chakras open, our bodies open, our consciousness opens and we become more connected to the infinite power of the universe. The universe becomes part of our being, and we then live open-heartedly and feel more empowered in our bodies. The universal force fuels us; we are no longer fueled by our fears. Divine inspiration leads us instead of crippling depression. We have angels on our side instead of anger in our hearts. The chakra system is our map to open our hearts and reach our full potential.

The first chakra is located at the bottom of the body. Some depict it at the perineum; others depict it at the anus. I have also heard the first chakra described as higher in women, because ours is at the cervix and men's first chakra is located at the perineum. Either way, the first chakra is located at the base of your body. The second chakra is located at your sex organs. The third chakra is located at your navel. The fourth chakra is located at your heart center. The fifth chakra is located at your throat. The sixth chakra is located at your third eye – on your forehead between your eyebrows. The seventh chakra is located at the crown or top of your head (see fig. 11.2).

THE SEVEN CHAKRAS

Figure 11.2

The chakras located lower in the body consist more of our instinctual, animal side, and the chakras located higher in the body consist more of our mental and spiritual side. Each chakra can have various levels of activity as it spins. Some can be more open than others. Some chakras, in certain situations, can shut down. When our chakras are open, they are functioning in a healthy way.

We can't live solely in our heads, in the clouds or in a state of spiritual bliss. Well most of us can't do that, right? Likewise, we can't solely operate on a physical level. Or at least it is not fun to do so. To make life more fulfilling, we need to have a higher consciousness, otherwise we would be no more evolved than an animal. I am not implying animals are not evolved, but we would not have higher intelligence if we didn't have these higher centers open, bringing in higher wisdom and evolving our consciousness as a species.

Ideally, to live a healthy, balanced life, you want to have all of your chakras equally open and balanced. However, often due to stress, belief systems and life challenges, the chakras get out of balance. You can have an underactive chakra. To compensate, other chakras may become overactive. If you do lots of computer work or mental work, you will lose the openness in your root, or first, chakra, for example. Various health problems can occur if the chakras stay out of balance chronically, either too active or too underactive. Illness can develop in the area of the chakra that is out of balance and in the gland associated with that chakra.

Each chakra is similar to a spinning wheel. When it spins clockwise, it is spinning in a direction that allows divine consciousness to flow through our bodies. When a chakra is spinning counterclockwise, our energy is blocked. We are resisting or not aware of something. Lack of awareness keeps us living in unconscious ways. Keeping the chakras unblocked and open is important. When all the chakras spin in a healthy direction and are open, you feel healthy and centered in your body. Let's discuss each chakra.

FIRST CHAKRA

The first chakra is also called the root chakra. It is located at or near the bottom of the body. It is usually depicted at either the perineum or the anus. The first chakra is about tribal connections and feeling a sense of belonging in the world, your community and in your life. It is your foundation. Having a community you can relate to and that gives you a sense of belonging, whether that community is your family or some other group, is important. The first chakra is about feeling safe in the world, feeling grounded and rooted. Someone who always moves may have a hard time establishing a healthy first chakra.

The root chakra addresses our most basic issues of survival, such as financial independence, food and feeling accepted by our "tribe." Having a sense of stability will keep your root chakra open. Life is never fully secure, but doing things that cause you to feel as if the rug is being pulled out from under you will destabilize your first or root chakra. Any big change in your life, such as a new job or moving to a new location, can cause your first chakra to shut down until you feel grounded again. That is why it is important to do things to ground yourself during transitional periods in your life. Any form of exercise, meditation or massage that is calming, slows you down and allows you to get out of your head and into your body will help nurture your first chakra. Lying on the earth in nature is a great way to feel grounded. Putting your feet on grass and feeling the sensation of connecting to Mother Earth is also a great way to "get rooted." A healthy first chakra creates an important foundation for the rest of the chakras.

SECOND CHAKRA

The second chakra is the sex chakra, located at the genitals. Often when working with the chakra system in public, for example in a yoga class, the teacher may explain that the second chakra is below the navel, but it is actually at the sex organs. The second chakra is considered to be below the navel and above the genitals because it isn't socially acceptable to put our hands over our genitals in public. However, it encompasses the whole area of your genitals and below your belly button. Your genitals hold lots of energy. Wouldn't you agree? They hold your creative life force energy. Why wouldn't there be a chakra dedicated to this area?

I call the second chakra the "sex, power and money" chakra. The second chakra is about your creativity. We can create another human being, we can create lots of money and we can create works of art. Definitely, each of us creates our own unique and individual lives. When we feel juicy and alive in the second chakra, we want to create. The problem is that we can create good or bad things. We can create situations that expand us, and we can create situations that bind and even destroy us. The second chakra is powerful, and it is important to bring greater awareness to how you navigate your second chakra.

Having sex with someone to create security is a good way to have your chakra spin in the *wrong* direction. You can't fool your second chakra. As a woman, your second chakra wants to be loved and adored, just as much as the rest of your body does. In our culture, there is a tremendous amount of conditioning in this chakra. A woman is supposed to be sexually attractive. A woman is also supposed to bear children and be a good mother. Also in our culture, a woman is supposed to be independent, autonomous and just as capable in a "man's" world.

Bringing more light and awareness to your second chakra is empowering. Sexual shame saturates our culture. Even if you learned to think of sex in a positive way, you still live in a culture saturated with sexual shame. There is no avoiding it. For us to create better relationships and lives, we need to heal the sexual shame stuck in the second chakra.

When you were young, what messages did you receive about being a woman? What did you learn about how a woman should conduct herself with the opposite sex? Did you receive a message that your femininity was a tool to get what you wanted? I call these, lovingly, "crotch contracts." Have you made any crotch contracts in your sexual relationships that are disempowering? Where have you sacrificed your most precious sacred space, and not in your highest good?

The second chakra is for us to learn to honor another and ourselves. Being sexual and sharing your genitals with another is a deep exchange. It is important to learn how to share in a way that honors you and the other if you want your second chakra to spin in a healthy direction.

THIRD CHAKRA

The third chakra is located at the navel. It is your power center and the seat of your emotions. The third chakra is about self-esteem, self-respect and knowing you are valuable. It is about knowing, no matter what is going on in your life, that you are a worthy human being.

When things go wrong, it is easy to beat yourself up and think you've done something wrong or that you're not good enough. Through those times, it is important to nurture and validate yourself. This will care for and support your third chakra.

Have you ever been in a situation where you feel a "pit" in your stomach? That is your third chakra talking to you. It is a time when you need to come to your own rescue and remind yourself that you are perfect, just the way you are. You need to know you are loved, and that you are good enough. The pit in your stomach is a call out to you to raise your self-esteem.

When you feel centered, confident and in charge of your life, you have a healthy third chakra. The third chakra is about learning to deeply, authentically and unconditionally honor yourself.

FOURTH CHAKRA

The fourth chakra is the heart chakra. It is located at the center of your chest. The heart is a powerful organ. It emits an electromagnetic field 40 to 60 times greater than that of the brain. The actual field created from your heart is far stronger than that created from your brain. The Heart Math Institute, an organization that studies the heart and emotions, has measured this energy and its effect on our well-being. The organization's mission is to facilitate a fundamental shift in health, well-being, and consciousness. They do phenomenal work. You can find them at www.hearthmath.com.

As we open our hearts, we develop compassion and raise our consciousness. The fourth chakra, simply put, is all about love. It is about learning to love others and ourselves in a balanced way. It is learning to give of ourselves in a way that is not self-sacrificial. It is about learning to not hold back, and to give of ourselves in a way that allows deeper connections with others. It is a tricky dance; I believe we are all here to learn about this dance.

I often hear people comment about how selfish someone is. *What is selfish?* My mother couldn't do enough for others. She was a beautiful and caring woman who died, I believe, earlier than she needed to. She gave so much of herself to others. She had five children, and was always available and ready to be of service to each of us. My mother was a great mom. I was lucky to have such an amazing and giving mother. There was one thing, though, that she didn't learn. She didn't learn how to give to herself as she so selflessly gave to others. She always put others in front of herself. She didn't know how to include herself in the equation of all the love she gave. She didn't know how to relax, open and receive. I believe many mothers, even though very loving, have these issues. The fourth chakra is not only about loving others; it is also about cultivating a sense of deep self-love.

The fourth chakra, the heart chakra, also teaches us to be more receptive. You are receptive when you have a neutral mind that is beyond judgment. An open heart means a neutral mind, no judgment. This is how you cultivate compassion.

The fourth chakra is the center chakra. There are three chakras above and three chakras below. The three chakras below are called the lower triangle. Many people spend much of their lives dealing with issues regarding the first three chakras. You have to understand the lessons of the first three chakras, the lower triangle, before you can truly open the fourth chakra, the heart chakra. Lower triangle issues are that of feeling safe in the world, being financially stable, having a positive relationship with sex, power and money, and feeling worthy and emotionally centered. Do these issues sound familiar? Most of us consistently confront issues of the first three chakras, and we never get above our bellies in our consciousness. The collective consciousness of our society plays out issues and dramas of the lower triangle (the lower three chakras). Not paying your bills (chakra 1), relationship drama (chakra 2) and not feeling good enough (chakra 3) are typical themes common in the lives of many in our culture.

The heart chakra teaches us to love others and ourselves no matter how much money, power or status they have. The fourth chakra teaches us about compassion and to love all beings, including ourselves, as equals.

FIFTH CHAKRA

The fifth chakra is located at the throat. This is the chakra of surrendering your will to *divine* will. It is about learning how to speak the truth, your truth, and how to speak from your heart.

We did not inherit a language that expresses itself eloquently through the heart. That is because we did not inherit a language that connects us to our needs and feelings. The language you speak, if you really analyze it, is disempowering. As a simple example, we often use the word "try." Begin to notice how often you hear people say they are going to *try* to do something. Trying implies just that, trying, but not completing it. Not only are we constantly "trying" to do something in our lives, we are also "having to" do lots of things as well. "Having to" implies that you're being forced to do something. You are not doing it from a place of choice. See if you can get "having to" out of your vocabulary. Instead, say, "I desire" or "I intend to." Can you stop "trying" and "having to" do things? Intending and desiring to do things will give you more energy and power to accomplish what you set out to do. When you do this, you will see how challenging it can be to avoid "trying to" and "having to." Shifting your words shifts the energy of your body.

These are two examples. Your words, whether they are spoken to yourself or out loud, have a powerful effect on your consciousness and how you feel. If you speak empowering words, you will move forward in the world with certainty and confidence. If you speak disempowering words, you will lack confidence and second-guess your actions.

Positive talk is extremely important for survival in this harsh world. Unfortunately, in many ways, our world is competitive and even predatory. If you can't be your own cheerleader and speak in a way that instills confidence in yourself and your life, then you will have a weak fifth chakra center, no matter how much support and cheerleading you receive from others.

You can also have a weak fifth chakra center if you hold back words by not sharing what you feel. Let's say you keep your mouth shut as a way to keep the peace. Or maybe you let your feelings come out sideways with drama, being over emotional, complaining or behaving like a victim. You are not speaking from your heart. The fifth chakra teaches us how to speak *our* truth in a way that is empowering, beyond blame and from the heart. It is the ability to speak your truth from your center. You can only do that if you have embodied your truth. It is when you intentionally use "I" instead of "You," as discussed earlier.

Using embodied "I" statements is authentic heart-centered communication. It creates a healthy throat chakra. It is not selfish, and it doesn't mean that you only care about yourself. It is direct and honest. It is empowering to your body and soul.

Be aware of this and start to notice when you are "You-ing" someone. What you are doing is playing victim and giving your power (energy) away. Instead, use "I" statements that express, in the moment and in the body, real-time reality. Examples would be: "I don't feel safe" or "I am hurt" or "Ouch; that hurt my heart." When you speak in embodied "I" statements, you bring power back to your body's energy field. Using "I" statements in this context is empowering.

In order to use "I" statements as we are discussing, you have to tune into you. You can't use "I" statements if you are disconnected from your feelings. You need to be self-aware. If you say, "I feel hurt," it is your reality. The other person may not like it, but they are not going to defend themselves. There is nothing to defend. You haven't attacked. You are simply stating what is going on with you in that moment. If you say, "*You* hurt me," everything changes. The other person can easily become defensive. You are also stating an opinion, and not necessarily a reality. You, again, are giving away your power. See if you can start to express yourself in a way that is closer to what you are experiencing in your body (your truth, not an opinion), and put it in words. "I am sad, I am mad, I am happy!" Bring all the energy back to you. Speak your truth from your heart, and your throat chakra will be healthier for it.

SIXTH CHAKRA

The sixth chakra is located at the third eye, the space just above and between your eyebrows. This is your third sight, or sixth sense. It is your intuitive guide and guardian. You can strengthen your third eye by closing the other two. We think what we see in the world with our two eyes is reality, but might it be possible that true reality can only be seen through our third eye? This chakra allows us to see beyond the day-to-day world. It is our spiritual connection. It brings the mystical into the mundane, making life a bit more divine.

The sixth chakra connects us to truth. What is truth? What is your truth? Because of our cultural and societal conditioning, many people do things for approval or to gain cultural acceptance. A big one is having kids. I have heard people say, "I thought you were supposed to grow up and have kids." They didn't consider that they had a choice in the matter. They thought, "This is what you do; you have kids when you grow up." Once they have children, they realize the huge responsibility associated with being parents. And maybe they aren't really into raising kids. Or maybe they didn't choose a good partner to share the responsibilities. Or maybe they did it because they wanted someone to love them. I pray for the day when our culture supports bringing children into the world more consciously.

This is just one example of how your truth gets covered up. Maybe you go to college and major in business, but what you really want to study is art and psychology. Layers of untruth wrapped around you keep you from making decisions from your authentic self. You let opinions, expectations and even fear influence you in your decision instead of listening to your inner truth and letting it guide you.

We all do this to some extent. We are all connected. We all want to be accepted by others, and our relationships help us see who we are. They reflect back to us who we are. That is why knowing your truth can be a slippery slope. Knowing what is right for you and all concerned is not always easy. That is why it is important to keep the third eye open to help guide you.

Your third eye is your intuition. Everyone has intuition, whether it is developed or not. It is worth developing and trusting your intuition. When your third eye is open, your higher self guides you. You are connected to spirit. You are able to see the vicissitudes of life from a higher and broader perspective. You aren't easily caught up in life's drama.

Your sixth chakra, or third eye, is also your imagination. Albert Einstein said, "Imagination is more important than knowledge." Imagination is how manifestation happens. Your sixth chakra draws inspiration into your life. Inspiration is "In Spirit." When you feel inspired, you are guided by Spirit. It is important to pay attention to those times, and then use your imagination to magnify the inspiration and put it into reality.

When you don't know exactly what direction to go or what path to take, still yourself and call on Spirit. Allow inspiration to come through your third eye. Ask your higher wisdom to show you the way. Open your third eye, your sixth chakra, and allow divine guidance to come in. It is more powerful than logic to guide you through unclear times. The sixth chakra teaches us to trust and be guided by our inner knowing.

SEVENTH CHAKRA

The seventh chakra is also called the crown chakra, and it is located at the top of the head. It is the soft spot on a newborn's head. The baby just came from the spirit world and is still very connected to "heaven." As the baby matures, the soft spot closes and becomes bone, part of the skull. As adults, even though we don't have soft spots any more, we still have a connection to "heaven" or Spirit. The crown chakra allows us to draw divine energy into our bodies. It is our connection to Source. I believe when we die, our souls go out through the tops of our heads.

It is important and empowering to know a divine presence is always around you. It takes faith in whatever form, be it religious or non-religious, to know there is more beyond this life's experience and the mundane world. The crown chakra is your spiritual connection, whatever that is for you. You may be Jewish, Hindu, Buddhist, Catholic or none of the above. The crown chakra is not your religious orientation. It is related to your *spirituality* and connection to the all-knowing and universal forces.

In summary, by working through the issues of each chakra, you illuminate your body and open it up, which allows divine energy and light to flow through you more and more. This is our evolutionary process, becoming connected to that part of us beyond our physical body while still in our physical bodies. It is the process of inviting your soul into form so it can express itself. Understanding the chakras helps us do that.

MOVING YOUR BODY SPIRITUALLY

We have already talked about deep breathing. Another word for that might be exercise. If you really want to learn how to empower yourself in your body, then you need to go a step further in your exercise program.

What type of exercises are you doing? Are they masculine forms of exercise or feminine forms of exercise? I am not referring to football as compared to ballet. I am referring to forms of exercise that will move your spirit, get you out of your head, and get you into your body, more specifically, into your sensual body.

If you exercise with a goal or agenda in mind, for example, lose weight, burn calories, win the game, hit the target, reach the goal, then you are doing a masculine form of exercise. If you are exercising to feel and experience the joy of being in your body, then you are doing a feminine form of exercise.

Feminine forms of exercise will move your spirit, put you into your sensual body and allow you a deeper sense of self-acceptance than you have probably ever experienced through traditional forms of exercise. Feminine forms of exercise support you to feel the pleasure of being in a human body.

Here is a personal example of the first time I experienced the subtle pleasure of being in my body while exercising. I have always been physically active. I was in gymnastics when I was young, took dance classes, jogged in college and took and taught aerobics for many years. I worked out in the gym, pumped weights, walked on the treadmill and took aerobic and spin classes. You will rarely find me in a traditional gym now if I can help it. Once I felt what it was like to be IN MY BODY, I was no longer attracted to gyms. Please don't get me wrong. I am not against gyms. They can be supportive for many people and a great way to stay in shape and stay healthy.

For women especially, there is another way, a deeper, better, more sensually alive way. A way that will keep you fit and more sensually centered. My personal experience showed me this. I remember my typical gym activity was to walk on the stepper and either watch the news on TV (some disaster or drama that was going on in the world) or look at other women's bodies and think, "I wish I had her hips," or, "I wish I had her flat belly." I did this all while I was breathing deeply, unconsciously instilling disempowering thoughts deep into every cell in my body!

Though I didn't realize it then, now I know that wasn't nurturing my soul, my life force energy or anything for that matter. Once I found a better way, I didn't go back to that form of exercise. For me, the better way was yoga and sacred dance. In 1996, I began doing yoga. I remember going to yoga with the intention of getting a good physical workout. I would even leave the class when it was time for Savasana (lying down meditation). I remember thinking the meditation part of the class wasn't important. I had things to do. When meditation came, I would run out the door to get on with my day. Now I know better. It is the dessert of a yoga class. It is where rejuvenation takes place. Nonetheless, by doing the main part of the class, I found it extremely fun and I liked the teacher. I may have been taking it as a fun way to "work out" for a while. I followed along in the poses. I was physically fit and flexible, so I could do most all of the poses. I remember being in a pose, breathing deeply and, for the first time in my life, a feeling of bliss came over my body, much unexpected, where I sensed inner joy, love and acceptance of my body. Though brief, it was a profound and transformational experience for me.

It was different from runner's high and it was different from the endorphin high I experienced when working out. I sensed delight and pleasure of being in my body that I had NEVER experienced before through exercising all my life. Having had a long history of body image issues, this was a wonderful experience, and I wanted more. I have had many more. Feeling pleasure or delight IN my body, with me, in a nonsexual way has helped heal my body image issues. It has gently guided me to honor and respect my body on a deeper level.

Yoga was my first introduction to feeling blissful in my body, all on my own. As yoga became my discipline, I experienced the beautiful, sensual sensation of being present in my body and feeling good in my skin. I developed a sense of mastery with moving my life force energy as I practiced yoga. Yoga made me feel good. The lovely way I felt differed from the endorphin high I got before when working out. For me, "working out" was more of a driven, almost manic, desire to feel good and often a desire to burn calories. Many times, I worked out while counting calories or thinking about how much fat I was going to burn. Yoga has never been like that for me. Instead, it has been a journey of spiritual and sensual awakening, healing, and a tool to help me clear my mind, release emotions and experience overall well-being. Other forms of exercise may offer similar benefits. For me, yoga was the ticket. It made a huge difference in my life for awakening to my more sensual nature.

All types of yoga will support you as a woman to awaken your sensual body. All yoga can help you get out of your head and into your body, especially if the class isn't too "heady" and analytical. You may need more instructional types of yoga classes when you begin, but as you become aware of proper alignment, I encourage you to take classes that allow you to go inward and create your own proper alignment. Anusara yoga is a powerful type of yoga that will provide you with the proper alignment and support you in creating greater body awareness. I especially love Kundalini yoga for its ability to refine and lift sexual energy out of the groin and up the spine. It supports elevating our spirit and increasing our radiant body. It also works quite rapidly on elevating one's consciousness, since it involves lots of movement and breath, encouraging the Kundalini to move up the spine to our higher centers in the brain. I love Vinyasa flow for its ability to expand the awakened Kundalini energy and cultivate a sense of mastery with moving one's life force energy in a fluid way. Vinyasa flow, depending upon the teacher, can be a beautiful yoga for supporting a woman in connecting to her feminine strength, confidence and developing a wholesome, sensual connection to her body. I love Yin yoga because of its slow, deep nature that supports sensual surrender and calming the body. Yin yoga, on a physical level, is good for connective tissues such as the ligaments, tendons and fascia. On an emotional and spiritual level, it supports you to drop down into your body, let go of tension and connect to deep currents of dynamic movement in the body simply by slowing down, holding a posture and relaxing into it. What a great metaphor for how to live our lives in a more empowered way.

Try different types of yoga. See what you are drawn to. If yoga doesn't work for you, find a form of exercise that is not goal-oriented, calorie-counting, driven or competitive. Find something that allows you to expand your subtle energy field, be in the moment and connect more consciously with your body.

SACRED DANCE

Sacred dance, or free form dance, is another form of "feminine exercise." This is something you can do at home alone or you can take classes. "5Rhythms," developed by Gabrielle Roth, is a wonderful way to exercise your body in a feminine way. Gabrielle has been teaching movement since 1977, and has certified more than 300 teachers worldwide. There may be a class in your area where you can dance, sweat and unleash your soul. You can go to www.5rhythms.com to find out more.

Whether you have a class to go to or not, you can create your own sacred dance experience in the privacy of your own home, just as I did, after my date, instead of eating pancakes. Make a collection of your favorite music, and play it with the volume turned up. Let the vibrations stir through your body and begin to move. See what your body wants and how it wants to express itself through the rhythm of each song. Let your body and your being go on a ride of self-expression. Discover what moves are enjoyable for your body. Discover what expressions unlock energy and allow for an opening. Let your heart expand and your lungs become spacious. Let go of form, and drop down into feel. Allow your emotions to create energy in motion within your being.

Your own private expression of sacred dance can take place any time and for any length of time. You may want to put on only one song and let the song move through you to rejuvenate you in the middle of the day, wake you up in the morning or end the day after a long day's work. Let dance and the beautiful expression of your feminine form be part of your life.

Let your body and your being go on a ride of self-expression. Discover what moves are enjoyable for your body. Discover what expressions unlock energy and allow for an opening. Let your heart expand and your lungs become spacious. Let go of form, and drop down into feel. Allow your emotions to create energy in motion within your being.

If you find yourself judgmental of how you dance, be gentle with yourself. If you don't feel your movements are fluid, it could be because you need to free up energetic blocks in your body. They may come from times of inhibitions or perpetrations that left you in a contracted state. Dancing is healing; allow your movements to be whatever they are. If they are jerky, give the jerkiness your undivided compassion and love. Remember, you are in the privacy of your own home. No one is watching you. This is a dance with you and your energy. Get to know it. Become intimate with the free flow of energy in your body. Move to whatever level your body is willing and able. Each hip circle is a vote for self-liberation. Let your hips circle, shake and sway in a way to loosen and free yourself from any past hurts. Let your divine essence out. She has been caged up for too long. You will find this to be a wonderfully cathartic and expansive experience.

LISTENING TO YOUR BODY

If you want to empower yourself by loving your body, then you will need to listen to it. Your body talks to you all the time. Your body is similar to a little kid that wants your attention. It is important to listen to "her." If you don't listen, she will let you know in a bigger way than you want. She doesn't want to, but she will get sick or develop a disease to get you to listen to her. Your body needs you to stop and be with her. It is important to have a relationship with your body and learn her language. Listen and tune in to what she needs. Don't eat if your body doesn't want food. Check in and see if your mind wants food. Check in when you are becoming sexual with a new person, and ask your vagina if she is ready to have someone enter her. Listen to her, and honor what she wants—not what your mind or what the other person wants.

Do you listen to your female parts? When I refer to women's female parts, I use the word *Yoni.* Many women have not heard of this word, but are familiar with other words, many of which are not affirming. Yoni is a Sanskrit word that refers to female genitalia. Translated, the word means *sacred space.* Most of us, as little girls, never learned that we had a sacred space, and did not learn how to treat it as such. Many women are disconnected from their Yonis. If you are not in touch with the most private part of your feminine self and her needs, how can you be empowered as a woman? How can you listen to your body?

Your body has its own language, and if you don't listen to it, your health will be affected. Many people have grown accustomed to putting a halt to the language of the body and using pharmaceuticals instead. As discussed earlier on, not all pharmaceuticals are bad, but many can be overused. Also, these drugs are designed to manage symptoms, not heal imbalance. How easy is it for you to take a pill, even for a headache, instead of slowing down and relaxing your body to release the tension in your head?

I understand; sometimes life's responsibilities won't allow you to slow down. We live in a fast-paced world. Changing your lifestyle takes effort and requires making your body a priority. It may even seem impossible to slow down because of all your obligations. That is why it is easier to deal with body aches, pains and other body issues by taking a pill. As I said before, taking pharmaceuticals is like fixing the oil light in your car by putting duct tape over it. Though these drugs can soothe your body or relieve your symptoms, using them does not help you get to the core of what your body is telling you. If you take a pill, you are not listening to what is off or out of balance inside you. Instead the pill covers that imbalance up; it turns off the function in your body to let you know.

Yoni is a Sanskrit word that refers to female genitalia. Translated, the word means sacred space.

When you take pills you are putting duct tape over the mouth of your body's communication system. If you do this habitually, you will further disconnect from your body and your body's effort to communicate with you. You will lose the ability to sense what is going on. Symptoms are there for a reason. Symptoms are the body's way of saying something is wrong. If you get rid of the symptom, which is what pharmaceutical drugs do, and don't take time to look at what is causing the symptom, then you are not healing the body. Something underneath can be brewing that is far worse.

The biggest drug category prescribed in the United States is antidepressants. We are a society filled with many very sad individuals. It is important to be compassionate with ourselves and with each other. If you suffer from chronic depression, you are not alone. If you are willing to get the right support and change your lifestyle, you can shift your situation. You are not stuck. You are temporarily disempowered.

Why is our society so depressed? I believe we have lost our ability to feel, to sense the joy of being alive. We take life for granted. We have cut ourselves off from the source of goodness found in every cell in our body and every sacred breath we take in. We have lost our senses because we have stopped sensing ourselves. For many, going inward can be very scary, especially if we have unprocessed emotions, so we numb ourselves instead of delving into the unresolved fear and pain. We need to sense ourselves, and come back home to our bodies to experience good health. We need to be able to hold uncomfortable feelings with our love and shed light on them. This is a process. Seek someone to help you. My individual coaching can help you. You do not have to deal with these hard, scary feelings alone.

As mentioned earlier, breath, movement and sound are powerful practices that help you to be in your whole body and to relieve depression. Proper diet is also important. Our world has become toxic. What we eat isn't healthy, vital food. Fifty years ago, there was no such thing as non-organic. Now we have to pay extra for organic food. Manufacturers have denatured our food as well, so our bodies are taking in GMOs (genetically modified organisms). We want, even crave, something real.

If you are present in your body, then you will feel a tremendous amount of bliss and feel grounded and centered. It feels wonderful! I believe that depression, though it can be due to imbalances in the brain, is basically a state of not being present in your body. Instead, you are in your mind, bringing yourself quickly to insanity. If you want to be happy, you need to live in your whole body, not just in your head.

It is important to celebrate the sacredness and joyous nature of being alive and human. The body wants to do that. The challenge is that it takes a level of self-commitment and time to practice breath, movement and sound in whatever form you choose to stay connected to your body and the natural source of goodness accessible within you and all around you. Making that time takes determination and effort. It is much easier to get caught up in life's busy patterns and become disconnected. Our society is set up to support that disconnect. We simply don't have enough systems in place in society to keep us rooted, grounded and feeling whole as individuals.

I have been depressed, but I have never suffered from chronic depression. For that I am very grateful. I believe that is in part because I love to move my body and do lots of yoga, hiking and walking. I do a tremendous amount of deep breathing on a regular basis so that I don't let the toxic world build up inside me. At the same time, only you can know yourself, your history, your needs and even your demons. If antidepressants work for you now, in this part of your journey, consciously recognizing that is critical to empowering yourself. It is perfect to recognize that right now antidepressants help you and be grateful for that. From there you can decide if more self-love, deep breathing practices, yoga, healthy food, coaching etc. will provide what you need to rebalance your mental well-being.

LOVING YOUR FEMININITY

Because we live in a masculine-oriented world, it is common for women to deny their femininity. Because we have been in this type of world for so long, we don't realize how distorted it is. We don't realize we are denying our femininity. It is similar to a disease we have to heal from, men and women alike. Women have been plagued with the idea that they are somehow second-class citizens. We have been beset with the false notion that we are not good enough. In this masculine-oriented world, being born a female has made us second best. We have this planted deep into our psyche. Here is a perfect example.

Years ago, I was in a grocery store and a man bumped into me. Guess what my first reaction was? I said, "I'm sorry." I realized when the man bumped into me, he was not compelled to say *he* was sorry, so why was I? *He* bumped into *me*! Of course, he didn't do it maliciously. It was an accident.

Nonetheless, I was compelled to say I was sorry. Why?

How often do you say you are sorry when it is unnecessary? What are you sorry for? Are you sorry for being born female? You don't have to be sorry for being here. You are not in the way. You are not a bother. It is important for us as women to claim our space in the world, unapologetically. We belong here!

In her book, *Female Realities*, Anne Wilson Schaef writes about the original sin of being born female. Though many parents want to have a little girl, many girls are born, and one or both of the parents are disappointed. They wanted a boy, not a girl.

I am one of five siblings. We four girls have one brother (the oldest). I will always remember my mother telling us she wanted to have five boys. My older sister's name was supposed to be Matthew. Then I was supposed to be Matthew, and then my younger sister was supposed to be Matthew. Guess what? Matthew never arrived. Seven years later, my mother gave birth to another child. By that time, since we siblings were older, we all decided Steven would be a good name for the baby instead of Mathew. Well, Steven didn't arrive. When my sister Joanne was born, she came home from the hospital without a name. We were all so sure she was going to be a boy that we hadn't prepared a girl's name!

How common is this phenomenon? Were you fully accepted as a little girl when you were born into this world? Maybe that's where "I'm sorry" comes from. Maybe that is why we don't fully embrace, claim and celebrate our femininity.

Make a choice not to be sorry in life, and you will feel more empowered! Make a choice to embrace your femininity as sacred, and you will heal yourself, your relationships and the world. Let's look at one tremendous way to empower yourself as a woman.

LOVING YOUR MENSTRUAL CYCLE

Having a menstrual cycle is a normal, natural and healthy part of being a woman. If you are no longer cycling, I encourage you to read this section anyway, as it may add perspective to your current femininity and to your past relationship with your cycle. Loving your menstrual cycle is paramount for embracing your femininity and empowering yourself as a woman. How do you feel about your menstrual cycle? Do you look forward to it every month? Do you hate it? Does it bring you down in a way that is painful, non-productive or disempowering? Does it control and overtake you when it arrives? Do you experience cramping? Does PMS have such a strong hold on you that you create drama in your relationships before you start your period?

As a woman, we have all experienced some level of discomfort with our periods. Our medical profession treats it as a problem, and the advertising world treats it as something that needs to be sanitized. To reclaim your body as sacred, you need to make peace with your period. Shift whatever you need to shift so that when your moon cycle comes, it is a celebration of your womanhood and your power. Because that's what it is!

If you are not feeling that, then you have been misled. It is not "the curse," which it was commonly called in the past. No more, women! Your moon cycle is sacred!

You hold within you the primal creative life force energy. Every month, you get a physical reminder that you have the power to create. You also are reminded that you have the power to cleanse. Your uterus sloughs off old energy, and you release that which you don't need. Your beautiful feminine body has the internal ability to cleanse every month in cycle with the moon. Men do not have this ability. This is very powerful!

As a woman, we are receptive, the "inney," which also means we can be the garbage collector of others' emotions. Women have a natural ability to be empathetic, to tune into other people and know what is going on with them. This is an important feminine quality needed for our vulnerable offspring. It is a beautiful quality, which comes with much responsibility. It needs to be balanced with self-awareness; otherwise, we can easily get lost in another and forget who we are. It is easy for women to become consumed by children and their needs, or an intimate partner and his or her needs. Women can easily fall into the behavior of people pleasing in order to make those they are close to happy. Does this sound familiar to you?

With receptivity comes more responsibility or need for greater awareness.

With receptivity comes more responsibility or need for greater awareness. Synonyms for *receptive* are words such as open-minded, persuadable, accepting, swayable and a pushover. With receptivity comes the risk of being swayed in a direction that may not be in your best interest.

Your monthly cycle, and the pressure that builds up right before your period, is a regulating mechanism for you to become aware of what you are receiving or allowing into your life. Do you allow people, places and things in that are life-affirming? Or do you let them rob you of your power? Do you receive input (opinions and direction) from others, when you really need to be guided by your own inner knowing and awareness?

PMS is a necessary pressure that builds up inside you to help you develop your authentic feminine strength and feminine confidence. It will help you develop your authentic feminine voice and ask for what you need. Without this extra pre-menstrual pressure, you might not have the courage to voice yourself. Right before your period, a situation in your life or a relationship might become unbearable. Has it become unbearable because there is something you need to look at and voice?

The important point is that you don't have to create drama, make people around you miserable or stay in silence and make yourself miserable. PMS is a time to see what you need in order to create more balance and life-affirming situations for yourself.

Know that after you ovulate and before your period is a great opportunity for you. During this time, things often come up that your soul wants you to address. These things surface for a reason. Your cycle's internal uterine buildup of blood is pushing you to express your feminine voice and empower yourself. Your emotions will surface and be your guide. It is up to you to use your emotions and this time wisely. The pressure cooker is on for a cycling woman. Whatever needs to be cleared and cleansed from your energy field and psyche is there to be released. See this time as sacred. Are you willing to take this time and use it wisely to enhance your life? It is not easy, through all the emotions, to see everything clearly. Getting the proper coaching and support can help tremendously. My coaching often involves helping women navigate their emotions to gain clarity and communicate confidently. I help women honor their emotions instead of hiding or repressing them. The point is that your cycle is sacred and can be a help instead of a hindrance.

As a woman, it is easy to let your emotions take hold of you. Your emotions can be your power—or your downfall. As mentioned earlier, under your strong emotions are unmet needs. The most powerful people on the planet know their needs and know how to get them met. A woman's nurturing nature and ability to care for other's needs makes it difficult to stay centered in her own needs. The ability to care for another, if we are not grounded in self-love, leaves us vulnerable to making others' needs a priority. There are life situations and times when you have to make another person a priority. Such times are when loved ones arrive and when loved ones leave, in other words birth, a new child, and death, someone passing away, or when a loved one is extremely ill. Nonetheless, self-care during this time should not be neglected. As a lifestyle and way of life, making others' needs a priority over yours weakens the fiber of your being. I believe creating a balanced flow of giving and receiving keeps us healthy and empowered.

Going back to the 4N process (Notice, Name, Nurture and Need) will help you develop your authentic feminine strength and confidence, express your needs and use PMS as a time to understand how you can create a more empowered you. It doesn't have to be a time of mayhem, drama, destruction or a time where you unconsciously give yourself permission to treat others with no regard or respect. Nor does it have to be a time when you hold things in and let your emotions fester into disease in your body.

What are your attitudes about your femininity, your womb and feminine parts? Many women have them removed; they can't wait to get their feminine parts out of their body. They have suffered with pain due to endometriosis, excessive bleeding or fibroids. Hysterectomies are routinely performed for different reasons such as endometriosis, fibroids, prolapsed uterus, cancer, chronic pelvic inflammatory disease and chronic pelvic pain. There could be many reasons why a woman has rejected that part of her. This is a complex matter, however we don't live in a feminine-friendly or womb-wise world. These women do the best they can in their situation. I am sure each woman has her own story, told or untold, conscious or unconscious, of how she feels about her feminine parts, and especially her sexual expression.

Sexual abuse causes women to have deep negative programming regarding their female anatomy. Sexual abuse is more common than most realize. It is a part of our culture that is not often discussed. Fortunately, that is changing, albeit far too slowly. Often when sexual abuse is present, it is rooted deep in the family structure. The behavior is passed down. How many little girls didn't know they had a vagina until Uncle Bob trespassed into their sacred space, for example? I want to stress, this is more common than we know. When this little girl grows up, the abuse may affect her ability as a woman to receive pleasure, have a wholesome feeling about her genitalia and feel comfortable with or clear about her sexuality.

Yonis are often mistreated unconsciously. How many women have been crawled on and squirted into, only to have the assailant roll over and fall asleep? I hate to sound so crude, but I want to make a point. What woman hasn't been sexually abused in this womb-neglected world? The majority of women have experienced at least some form of sexual un-pleasantries where they cater to his needs and put theirs second. This is all due to a woman's lack of knowing that her Yoni is hers, and it is worthy of deep pleasure. It is sacred and precious. I believe all women are healing from this lack of knowing.

Inherent in our society is a negative stigma towards our genitalia for both men and women. Did the shame we hold in our genitalia start in the Garden of Eden when we took from the tree of knowledge? Ah, and yes, of course, Eve was to blame. Women have been used as the fall guy (gal) for being what they are naturally: succulent, juicy and deliciously irresistible. Sexy is a sin in our culture. Women carry this negative stigma and sin of being sexy due to the sexual objectification we live with in this less-than-sexually-conscious world.

Words such as "dirty" or "nasty" are words often projected onto women's bodies and Yonis. We have taken them on as our own, but the Yoni knows better. The Yoni knows who she is. She will never lose her identity. You may lose your way because of living in a womb-neglected world, but not your Yoni. The Yoni will always know her place in the universe and she will always recognize that it is a place of divine power. Your Yoni can show you the way. You just need to connect with her. It is up to us individually as women to change all the negative perceptions about our femininity. It first starts with changing perceptions within yourself and the relationship you have with your Yoni.

Working with your blood is a good way to develop pride in your menstrual cycle and to build genital appreciation and genital confidence. For generations, women have been programmed to think having their period is something they need to hide, cover up or be ashamed of. It has not been a subject often talked about in the past. I believe that is changing. Women need to talk with each other and out in the open about this most mystical and magical biological process and blessing. It is something to praise, exalt and celebrate. Your menstrual blood would otherwise have been a nest for new life. Within the blood is the life-giving essence. It should, as should all feminine bodily fluids, be treated as divine.

You might be cringing at the mention of working with your blood. "What do you mean?" you might ask. If your reaction is judgment or disgust, I suggest you look at why that is coming up for you. In prehistoric times, men saw women bleed and not die from it. The women carried on as usual. This was probably a mystical phenomenon for the prehistoric male. From a prehistoric male's point of view, if he bled that much he would surely die. Women did it regularly with no ill effect. I can imagine how much this must have amazed men. I am sure cavewomen were proud of their menstrual cycles in those times. It was a display of their power.

If you have not already done so, begin to embrace your menstrual cycle and your blood. Understand that when you have your period, it is one of the times you are most in your sacred power as a woman. Your menstrual scent gives off pheromones that say, "I am powerful; I hold within me the ability to carry life." Also, when you ovulate, your body is saying, "I can create another life." Tap into the awareness of your female body communicating this. Even if you have never had, or will never have a child, understand the power of your amazing feminine form and its ability to create. Have you embraced that?

Your cycle is also a time to slow down and become receptive to this sacred feminine process. I always loved my periods and rarely had negative symptoms to deal with. I never had cramps. I believe it was largely due to my positive attitude about my period. I deeply understood how sacred my feminine flow was. I grieved when I approached menopause.

Whether you have a challenging menstrual cycle or not, take this time to slow down and rejuvenate. We are often "on the go." A part of making peace with your menstrual cycle is to take this time every month, as a ritual for yourself, to slow down and drop into your feminine. This may be, as it was for me, hard to do. When you do, you'll find it easier to develop positive programming around your period. It is your *rest* time. It isn't your time to be *ill*. It is your time for you. It is a time to go inward. It is a time of relief because you are releasing any built-up energy that your body wants to release. You are being rejuvenated. Take advantage of this time as much as you can. Make time for yourself each month; journal, take a walk, sit and hold your belly, and most importantly, collect your blood and make use of it. Don't just let it go down the toilet or soak in a tampon that gets discarded.

I didn't start collecting and using my blood until I was forty years old. I don't remember how I concluded it was an important thing to do. I believe it was because I faced living by myself as a single woman in a big house after having been with my husband for eleven years. It was going to be an adjustment. The typical thing for a woman living alone would be to get an alarm system. I enlisted a different power. I had heard of the idea of women's menstrual blood being powerful. I had my period right after my husband died. My body magically knew it was time to release.

My mother had flown into town, intuitively knowing she wanted to be there for me when he passed. She was right on. She flew in during the day, and he passed that night. She and I helped him cross over in what I experienced as a birthing process. Heaven came into our home to get him, and heaven didn't leave. I felt an angelic presence in the house and in my mind's eye saw a white bubble of light over the whole property. I believe I was guided to work with my blood, and I knew the mystical powers of my menstrual cycle. I decided to collect my blood and put it around my property for protection. Though grieving, I was in an altered state of awareness of the spiritual kind. I was sad and exhausted, however I was relieved because my husband was no longer in pain. I believe I was feeling his exalted state.

I used menstrual washcloths, which I put into a rubber dishpan that was half-full of water. The blood drained off the cloth, and into the water. My mother accompanied me while I prayerfully walked around my property, blessing the grounds with my blood. My mother, a more conservative woman, stood by my side as we walked around my property. Though she wasn't familiar with such a thing, her Yoni had the knowing, and she was there to support me in the ceremony.

After that, I always used my blood for good things. Mainly I used it to protect me in my home. I watered plants with it as well. I have never publicly told people about this. I have told my close friends if it came up. Otherwise, it was a sacred monthly ritual for me. I want to share this intimate practice with you, because I feel working with your blood is a well-kept secret that women need to know about. It's not unnatural. This ancient wisdom needs to come back into a cycling woman's everyday life. It will support you as you find peace with your body, your femininity, your connection to the divine and Mother Earth.

Collect your blood every month and bless the earth with it, protect your property, or do whatever creative thing you can think of to use your womb power to create a better life for yourself and the world.

LISTEN TO YOUR BODY'S MESSAGES

Your body is a magnificent piece of art with all of its interconnected biological functions. The body has divine intelligence, and always wants to move toward a state of perfect health. It requires only the proper environment to enable it to move towards its natural state of perfect health.

If you want to love your body and feel empowered in it, commit to listening to your body and the messages it has for you. If you have any health challenges, ailments or pain in your body, then tune into them. Know that a belief or behavior probably caused it. Uncover the source of the *Dis Ease* that is causing your body to be out of balance. You may have to deal with the health issue, ailment or pain a bit longer than if you took pills from your medical doctor, but it is well worth it. In looking deeper and seeing what is behind the *Dis Ease*, you will develop a deeper relationship with yourself. Isn't that part of getting to know ourselves better?

Louise Hay is a spiritual speaker, writer and teacher. She has written wonderful books. She wrote a book that I absolutely adore, called *Heal Your Body*. In this little book, you can look up various ailments, and the book will give the probable thought pattern that created the ailment. It also gives affirmations to heal the negative thought pattern. This "little blue book" has been a great reference for me to help others and myself over the years.

Louise Hay's book is fun to bring to an intimate social gathering. You can look up each other's ailments and see what probably caused them. She also gives positive affirmations for each ailment. For fun, here are some causes she has in the book. Cold sores are festering angry words and fear of expressing them. Hip problems are fear of going forward, nothing to move forward to. Stiff neck is unbending bullheadedness. Constipation is refusing to release old ideas, being stuck in the past, and sometimes, stinginess.

The concept is that every disorder has meaning. Your body doesn't just get out of balance. Your body is talking to you. There is a reason why it is out of balance, and it is important for you to take time to figure it out. Healers, coaches, therapists and energy workers can guide you along the way. Ultimately, it is up to you to change thoughts, beliefs and behaviors that affect your health. If you listen to your body more and honor its messages, you will be healthier. You will deepen your relationship with your body.

You will grow profoundly, both emotionally and spiritually.

If you immediately turn to pharmaceuticals and continue to live as if nothing is wrong, then you will miss an opportunity to learn more about yourself. Take time to look at possible sources of the imbalance, and learn more about your body. Make any lifestyle or emotional changes necessary to create balance and health. Then, if you still need to take a pill, go ahead. At least first give yourself a chance to broaden and deepen the experience you are having in your human body. It is a vessel of the divine, a vessel for your soul. If you don't listen to it, then your soul won't want to be in it anymore. Your life will end. Listening to your body and its messages gives you an opportunity to live a more empowered life.

I am not an expert on all the physical/emotional connections of the body, though I have a certain level of understanding, and I am always learning more. There is much to learn in this regard, and I find it fascinating. I enjoy learning and understanding more about how the body is wired, emotionally, physically and spiritually. The point I am making is that your body is not separate from anything, especially your emotions. Everything in life, the body, and relationships is interwoven. Understanding this will help you deepen your relationship with yourself, especially any "blind spots" you may have. Your blind spots are your illnesses. They are places where you have an opportunity to grow. They are places inside you that need more love. Understanding the interconnectedness between you and everything around you will help you open deeper to love. Let your body be your roadmap for opening to love and greater awareness.

HEALTHY BOUNDARIES

Knowing how to establish healthy boundaries is how you establish healthy relationships. In order to establish a healthy boundary you need to be self-aware. Having a sense of self-esteem is also important because it gives you the strength and will to set healthy boundaries in the first place. If you are not used to setting healthy boundaries, learning to do so allows you to develop self-esteem. You are then able to have human interactions that are life enhancing instead of life depleting.

When you are aware of your inner world, your feelings and your needs, you are able to energetically protect yourself and refrain from inappropriately taking on other people's problems or issues as your own. You are able to express and communicate your needs to others in a productive and heart-centered way. You don't get pulled into something that isn't in your highest good or in the highest good of those around you. You are still loving and supportive, however, you maintain a clear sense of self, not falling prey to becoming a rescuer, being dominated, dominating or controlling others, being over-emotional, manipulative or losing yourself in relationship; qualities of a dysfunctional relationship that leave you feeling disempowered.

The way most women were raised, it is easy for us to take on other people's energy as our own. Anatomically, we were designed to bear children, be their caretakers, and nurture them. Those qualities can leave us vulnerable to becoming codependent if we haven't done the inner work to have healthy relationships and boundaries. Their needs become our needs, and our needs get buried. Have you ever lost yourself in a relationship? Have you ever sacrificed your personal needs for the needs of another to the point that is beyond normal self-sacrifice and caring? Have you ever looked to others for approval when you really needed to accept yourself? Imagine what that does to your body's energy field, let alone your identity and power. It is always good to give to others, but when you don't take care of your own physical, emotional and spiritual needs first, you are unable to give to others in a healthy way.

Relationships are everything. "Aho Mitakuye Oyasin" is a Lakota

Sioux term that means "All My Relations." It acknowledges our interconnectedness. Healthy relationships are inter-dependent rather than codependent. Others affect us, and we are all in relationship. Whether you are in a love relationship or not, you are "in relationship." You are in relationship with your parents, siblings and coworkers, to name a few. First, you are in relationship with yourself. If you want to have healthy relationships, it is crucial to have healthy boundaries. Practicing healthy boundaries enables you to maintain a healthy energy field around your body.

Unhealthy relationships lack the necessary amount of communication, cooperation and co-creation to make life enjoyable. Typically one person supports and even enables another's addiction or destructive behavior. They become codependent. They become the rescuer thinking they are being helpful. They define themselves and their sense of self by being pre-occupied with another's needs over their own.

Codependents are often victims. A victim needs a perpetrator. Energetically, the perpetrator dominates your energy field. Your energy field is contracting and becoming smaller. If you could see this on an energetic level, you would see a small energy field being overcome by a larger energy field. The larger energy field is not all of that person's energy. The perpetrator is "taking" your energy.

You can also take on other's emotions, become overemotional, erratic or agitated simply because you are connected to someone unable to express their feelings. In addition, it is possible to become enmeshed with another where your relationship lacks clear boundaries. Relationship dynamics can take on different energetic forms. In a love relationship, this is often the case. As a result, it takes a tremendous amount of self-love, self-nurturing and healthy boundary-setting to bring your energy field back to its normal and natural bright self. See the following illustrations for common examples of relationship energy dynamics. The last example, where each individual's uniqueness is honored, creates an environment for healthy relating (see fig. 11.6).

If you want to

have healthy relationships,

it is crucial to have healthy boundaries.

Practicing healthy boundaries enables

you to maintain a healthy energy field

around your body.

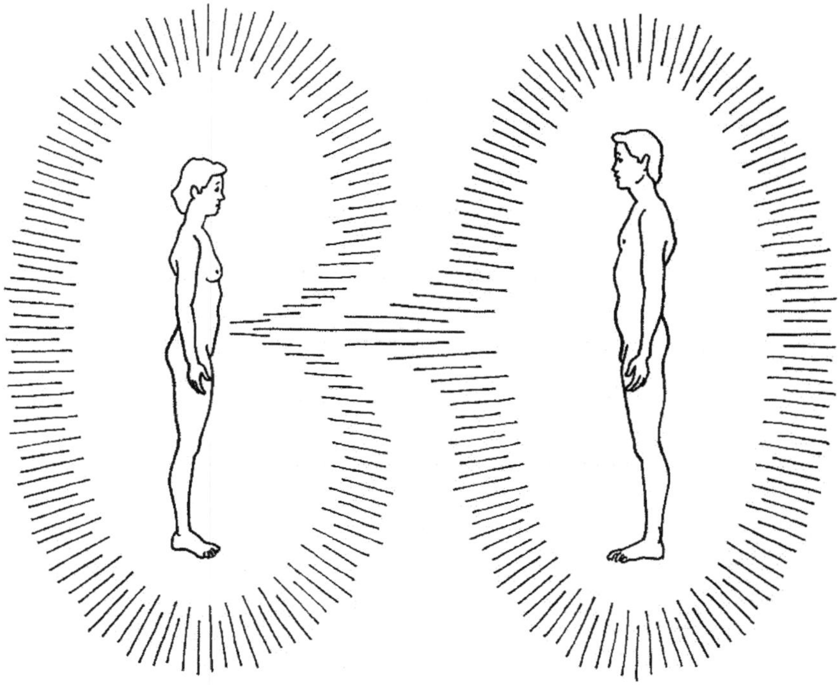

Figure 11.3

The person on the left is taking on the emotions of the other. This typically results in becoming over-emotional when the person on the right is unable to show emotions.

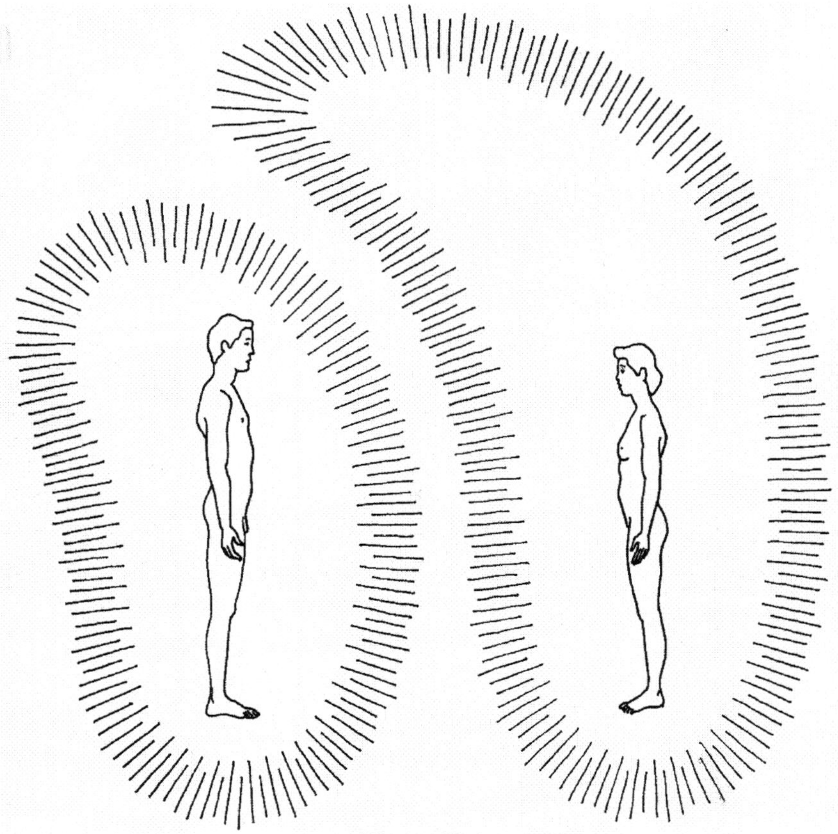

Figure 11.4

The person on the right is dominating the other, taking the other's energy as a way to feel powerful.

Figure 11.5

This is an example of unclear boundaries. You don't know where you end and the other person begins. This often happens when you "lose yourself" in a relationship.

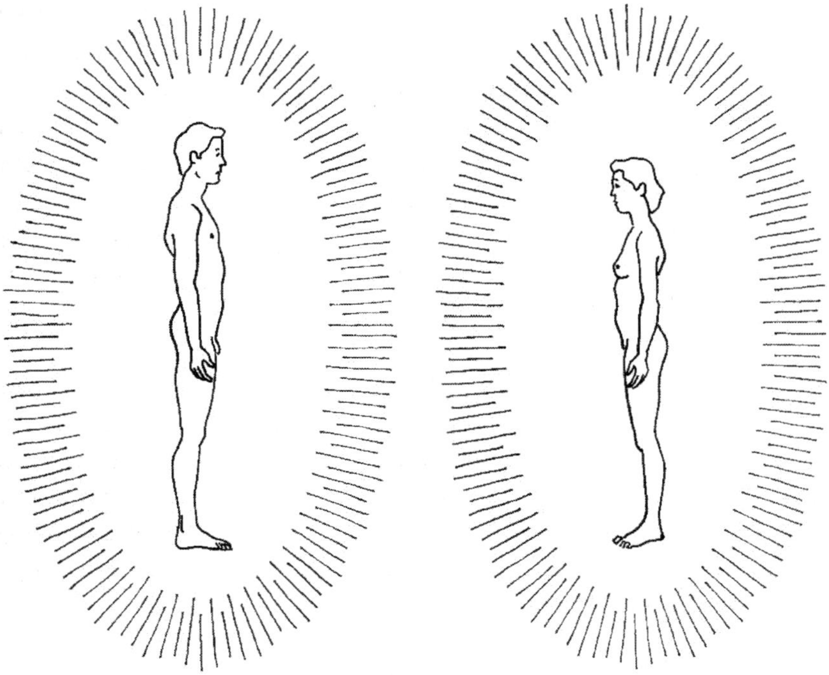

Figure 11.6

These two people have healthy boundaries; they mutually honor each other's opinions and uniqueness.

Establishing healthy boundaries can be challenging, but it is a must in order to keep your body's energy field bright, live in your truth and not lose yourself. One of the challenges is determining when a boundary becomes a barricade. What is the balance between self-care and caring for others?

It can be difficult to identify a healthy boundary. It is similar to walking a tightrope. There is a fine line between you and others, especially those close to you, because we are interconnected and learn from each other. That is why it is important to cultivate a sense of self and know how to be with your feelings and understand your core needs. Become aware of times when you overextend the energy you give to others. Become acutely aware of when you are having uncomfortable feelings. Don't run from them. Take time to be with your feelings and discover what your unmet needs are. The 4N process is an effective practice to learn if you want to have healthy, life-enhancing relationships.

Keeping the integrity of your energy and staying centered requires that you care for your energy just as you care for your body, your teeth or your hair. Try to recognize what happens when your energy shifts downward or contracts due to interactions with others. Take the necessary steps to go inward to discover and acknowledge your core need. Then voice your truth from your heart and energetically stay centered. This will keep your energy field in a state of integrity.

As you learn healthy boundaries and are able to get in touch with your feelings and the underlying core needs, your body's energy field will expand. You will develop compassion for yourself and others, radiating more heart energy. Heart energy is love energy, one of the most powerful energies on the planet. You will experience more joy in your relationships because you will have learned not to hold onto uncomfortable emotions and the associated dysfunctional behaviors that bring a relationship down. Your relationships won't become tainted and toxic. Your energy field will be bright, powerfully invincible and pure.

Most of us take a shower on a regular basis, if not daily. If we are healthy, we brush our teeth once, if not more, each day. When you move your body, and I mean exercise it in some form, is it like brushing away the buildup of daily life. So too, it is important to brush away daily tension on a regular basis. If you didn't brush your teeth, you would have tooth decay, bad breath and gum disease. If you never took a shower, you would have an unpleasant body odor and a layer of grime coating your body. Others might not find it very pleasant to be around you, and you probably wouldn't feel good in your body, either. The same happens if you don't cleanse your energy field on a regular basis using breath, movement and sound. Built-up tension, stress and emotions will cling to your body and energy field. You can easily become confused and lack clarity in your relationships. It is important to release this energetic buildup, even though you can't see it, in order to maintain mental clarity.

I teach a five-minute exercise I call the "Shake Out." It won't cure codependency or create healthy boundaries for you, but it is a fun self-care tool that supports self-awareness. It also helps you to clear your energy so that you can think clearly. It involves rapidly moving different body parts to shake off tension, stress and other people's energy. In a few short minutes, you can feel more alive by releasing tension.

When we are out in the world in daily life, our energetic interchange is similar to bumper cars. All of us bump up against each other energetically. We each have our own agenda, things we want to do in our lives. You may experience someone's agenda bumping up against your desires. This creates resistance for you in reaching your goals. This is part of life. Our auras, the energy fields around us, can contract and become, in a sense, dented. We can then feel out of balance.

The Shake Out is a quick, easy and fun method to care for and support your energy field. It will quickly put you in an expansive, instead of contracted, state. It is one of many tools to help you move through life in a more balanced way. You can find it on YouTube by typing in "Anna-Thea Shake Out." Look it up, try it and enjoy the benefits. It will have you feeling lighter and brighter in a few minutes.

Do the Shake Out when you feel stressed. I am there for you! In five quick minutes, I will have you breathing deeply with a smile on your face. Enjoy!

ENLIVEN AND ILLUMINATE YOUR BODY

Understanding and listening to your body, and becoming aware of your inner world, is part of how you create healthy boundaries. Enlivening and illuminating your body also helps you to create the necessary sensing of self and self-esteem to set healthy boundaries. Most of what we have talked about so far are things that will enliven and illuminate your body. Let's take it a bit further. I want to give you a few more tools you can use in your daily life to help you illuminate your soul within your body.

HANDS ARE YOUR HEALERS

My hands have been my healers. "HANDS" is an acronym I created. It stands for Healing, Awakening and Nurturing Done Sensually. It is important to have a kinesthetic relationship with your body. It helps you feel more centered and grounded. It helps you to be less in your head and create a deeper sense of self. How often do you make a kinesthetic connection with yourself? If you want to feel empowered in your body and love it, making physical contact with yourself is a good way to support that.

We live in a touch-deprived world. There are many lonely people who don't have anyone to touch them. Getting involved in a sexual situation you know is not in your best interest because you feel deprived of touch is not a good idea. Touch is important and necessary in order to have a healthy body. You can't always rely on someone else to satisfy that need. That is why having a kinesthetic relationship with your body is important.

Your hands are extensions of your heart. Everyone has the ability to send healing heart energy through their hands, even if they have never consciously done it. Become aware of the energy that emanates from the palms of your hands. A good way to do this is to rub your hands together rapidly, and then pull your palms about five or six inches apart, facing each other. You will feel the energy created between your two hands. Awaken the healer within you by touching yourself. Spend time with your hands on your body with the intention of sending healing energy deep into your being. In doing so you will create, what I call, vibrational nourishment.

CREATING VIBRATIONAL NOURISHMENT

Vibrational nourishment is an art form of developing energetic nourishment for your body. Just as healthy food nourishes your body, good energy nourishes your body and soul. This is an art form worth developing. The nourishing energy increases the vitality of our bodies and heals any emotional need to eat (or engage in other obsessive behaviors). Vibrational nourishment practices are soothing practices for the feminine soul. They will fill you up with good, healthy, positive energy, and they will help you reach *in* instead of reaching *out* in an unhealthy way to food, people, places and things. These vibrational nourishment practices nurture your life force energy.

By nourishing your body with these practices, you fill yourself up with beautiful, positive energy. This beautiful energy then shines out from you. In our world, the societal ideal of a woman's youthful beauty is a sought-after commodity. Youthful looks tend to have a short shelf life, which is okay. Love yourself and your body's unique beauty in every stage of life. Learn to allow your inner light and beauty to shine through by creating vibrational nourishment in your life.

Vibrational nourishment practices are a way to put love, aliveness and connection into your feminine body. They are a way to receive what you so readily give to others… nourishment. This is a way to turn your innate ability to nurture and nourish inward.

Learn to allow your inner light and beauty to shine through by creating vibrational nourishment in your life.

Our vaginal anatomy lends us to the desire of wanting to be filled. As sensual beings, energetic nourishment satisfies our need to feel sensually fulfilled and nourished. Vibrational nourishment practices awaken our ability to receive pleasure. Before we can feel pleasure, we need to feel relaxed. These exercises relax the feminine spirit. They are ways of living, things you can do, and behaviors that will give you a healthy way to fill yourself up instead of looking for someone or something to fill you up, e.g., a man, shopping, or food. These are sacred, sensual pleasure practices. Let your personal sensual practice be your savior. There are many vibrational nourishment practices you can use to enhance your relationship with your body. The following are a few that I highly recommend making part of your life. They will help to enhance your relationship with your body.

EXERCISE: HEART, HANDS, BELLY AND OVARIES

A simple way to make contact with yourself and activate a "healing hands" relationship with yourself is to put one hand on your heart and one hand on your belly. I like to put my left hand on my heart and my right hand on my belly. The left side of your body is the feminine side. The right side of your body is the masculine side. Your left hand is your receptive hand, and your right hand is your giving hand. When you put your left hand on your heart, imagine inhaling and receiving the love from your heart. Then with your right hand on your lower belly, imagine all that love going down your right arm, then deep into your belly. Do this with intention. When you go to bed at night, this practice of one hand on your heart and another hand on your belly is a nurturing and soothing practice as you end your day and begin to fall asleep.

You can also place both hands over your ovaries and send your ovaries healing energy. I believe this is a powerful exercise for ovarian health and a way to nurture your creative feminine essence. The palms of the hands are powerful; healing energy emanates from them. To locate your ovaries, place your thumbs on top of your belly button with your fingers facing down toward your Yoni. With the index fingers touching, let the rest of your fingers line up, slightly separated, in the direction of your Yoni and on your belly. Where your baby fingers are, is where your ovaries are. Reposition your left and right palms on your left and right ovary. You can rub your hands together first to create more heat. Take a big breath, and as you exhale, consciously place the palms of your hands on your ovaries as you visualize your hands sending healing energy deep into your ovaries. This will nurture your feminine creative life force energy (see fig 11.7).

A third simple kinesthetic exercise to do with your hands is to place one hand on your belly above your belly button and the other hand on your belly below the belly button. In this fashion, you are embracing your entire belly area, digestive tract and internal organs. There is a lot going on in our bellies. Placing your hands on your belly this way, with conscious awareness, creates a beautiful connection between you and your third chakra, the chakra of self-esteem. This is an empowering and nurturing exercise.

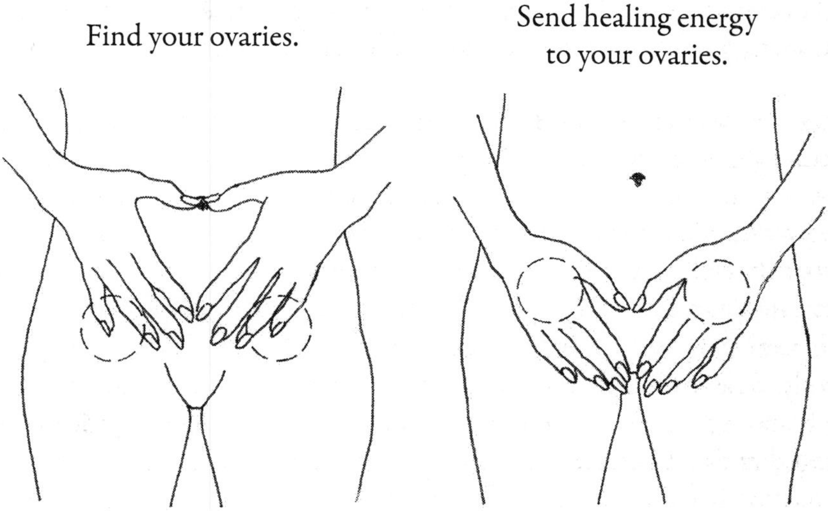

Figure 11.7

These simple practices, when done with the intention of sending healing energy inward, promote self-awareness, deeper relaxation and a more loving relationship between you and your body. Your hands can help create intimacy with yourself.

EXERCISE: BELLY BREATHING

Belly breathing is a wonderful vibrational nourishment practice for nurturing your body. To belly breathe, sit or lie down. I love lying down because it is very relaxing and a bit more sensual, but sitting is also very good. Either way, when you do this breathing, it is best to put your hand on your lower belly. Often when we breathe, we don't fully take in oxygen. Belly breathing allows you to take in a full breath and bring it all the way down into the belly. If you look at babies, you will notice this is how they breathe. When they breathe, their whole belly fills. That is one of the ancient secrets of staying young. Maintaining your youth requires breathing like a baby.

As women, we are programmed to keep our bellies in. Every woman would probably like to have a perfectly flat belly. But if you are a woman, you are designed to have a belly. It is part of being a woman. It doesn't mean that belly breathing will make your stomach stick out more. It just means that you need to get used to the idea of giving yourself permission to have your belly distend. Place one of your hands on your lower belly even while you are reading this and begin to breathe all the way down into your belly. Fill your lungs up and then fill up your lower belly. See how much oxygen you can bring all the way down to your lower belly. See how much you can make your belly fill up with your breath. You can even hold it for a moment and then let it go. Do this for a while and see what effect it has on you. This is the technique I use when working with clients to help them get out of their minds and be in their bodies. It is a powerfully relaxing breath. It is a powerful tool to help you create an environment for listening to your body.

EXERCISE: INNER SMILE – ILLUMINATING YOUR ORGANS

Another tool to enliven your body and create vibrational nourishment is called the inner smile. This is a well-known Taoist practice. It is a simple, yet profound, practice. I am not a certified Taoist practitioner or teacher. However, when this practice was introduced to me, it felt nurturing to my being. I have continued this simple yet powerful practice for many years in my own version, which I would like to share with you. The practice involves you smiling inward towards your organs, cultivating and sending them kind regard and gentle loving kindness. You can do this by imagining that you are sending gentle kindness into your body or a certain part of your body. You can also do this by placing your hand on that area of your body. This beautiful practice of illuminating your inner world helps enhance your awareness of subtle energies in your body.

This inner awareness is an illumination process. You are bringing conscious awareness into your internal organs, creating a connection with them. You are illuminating yourself from the inside out with your smile. You are bringing the inherent healing energy that emanates from your hands deep into your body. At the same time, you are bringing your mental attention there. This enhances the mind-body connection and self-compassion.

When you do the inner smile, turn your lips up slightly to create a gentle smile on your face as you send kind regard into the area you are focusing on. A great vibrational nourishment practice is the inner smile to all of your internal organs while lying in bed first thing in the morning. This is a wonderful practice, especially if you are the type who has a hard time getting up in the morning. Use this time to cultivate self-love and vibrational nourishment. You can begin in any order. I like to start at my heart. You can be as creative as you like. Here is an example of a sequence. You can vary it. Make it part of your morning waking ceremony.

Inner Smile Sequence

Place your hands on your heart. Begin to smile down into your heart, sending gentle kindness deep into your heart. As you inhale, puff up your heart. As you exhale, let your heart melt. Turn your lips up with a gentle smile as you continue to do the inner smile to your heart, sending it kind regard. You can stay focused on your heart for as long as you like. Once you feel the warmth of your hands and the inner smile in your heart, or when you are ready, move your hands to your breasts. Let the palms of your hands melt into your breasts, with the center of the palm of each hand covering your nipples. Your nipples are like sponges; they will absorb the warmth you give them. Begin to send gentle loving kindness into your breasts and into your lungs with your inner smile. Once you feel the warmth of your hands radiating deep into your breasts, and the inner smile deep into your chest and lungs, you can, when you are ready, move down to your liver and right kidney.

Since kidneys are a bit harder to reach when you are lying in bed, I find it easier to do the liver and right kidney at the same time. Lean your body slightly over to your left side, exposing the right side of your body. Place your left hand just below, or on, your lower right ribcage. This is where your liver is located. Place your right hand on your right kidney, which is located at the mid-part of your back, on the right side, at the level of your waistline. With this position, in effect, you are cupping your liver and right kidney. Stay there and smile down into your liver and your right kidney, sending kind regard into both organs. Send appreciation for all they do for you. As you inhale, you can puff up your liver and right kidney, and as you exhale, let them relax. Feel the healing energy being absorbed into your organs.

You don't have to force anything. This is a relaxing experience. You will feel the warmth of your hands penetrating deep into the right side of your body. It should feel nourishing and calming.

When you feel complete on the right side, you can do the same on the left side of your body, where your spleen and left kidney are located. Take your right hand and place it on the left, front side of the body just below, or on, the left lower ribcage. Then place your left hand on your left kidney at the mid-back. You can lean your body a little to the right, so the placement of your hands is comfortable. Stay there and continue the inner smile to your spleen and your left kidney. Again, as you inhale, you can puff up the organs, and as you exhale, allow your inner smile and kind regard to penetrate deep into your spleen and kidney.

From there, you can place your hand over your navel and send kind regard into your navel and pancreas. The pancreas is located deep in the abdomen, partially behind the stomach. The other part nestles in the curve of the small intestines, located deep behind the belly button and to the left a bit. The pancreas is part of the endocrine system, and is in charge of regulating the insulin in our bodies. It processes sugar. It is involved in digesting the sweet things we eat. If you have a sweet tooth, then your pancreas works overtime. Smile deeply into your navel and send gentle loving kindness into your pancreas. Give it gratitude for all the hard work it has done in its life of digesting the sweets you indulge in.

Then place your hands on your ovaries. Your ovaries are located near your groin (see Figure 11.7). Place the middle of each palm of your hand over each ovary. Let the energy from your hands radiate gentle kindness into each ovary. Feel the warmth of your palms as you bless your ovaries and give them a nice inner smile. Your ovaries hold your creative life force energy; from them spring forth ovum to create new life. As you send loving kindness to your ovaries, your creative energies are awakened. Feel the creativity flowing in your pelvic bowl.

To finish this vibrational nourishment exercise, take all your luscious feminine creativity and begin, with one hand, to circle, counter-clockwise, around your belly, circling from the bottom of your belly over to the left, then up to the top of your belly, across to the right side of your belly, and down again. Keep circling in this counter-clockwise direction for at least nine circles. Visualize your hand radiating healing energy deep into your belly as you make the circles, clearing and cleansing away any stuck energy as you continue to circle counter-clockwise. Then reverse the direction and begin circling your hand in a clockwise direction. Taking your hand across the top of your belly from right to left, down the left side of your belly and then across the bottom of your belly over to the right, up the right side of your belly and back across the top over to the left. Visualize divine healing energy penetrating deep into your belly as you move your hand clockwise around your belly.

When you have completed a minimum of nine clockwise circles, end by resting your hands on your lower dantien. The lower dantien is one of three energy centers from the Taoist system. The dantien centers are for storing life force energy or chi and for cultivating vitality. The lower dantien is located about three finger-widths below your belly button. Rest your hands in this location, with your left hand on top of your right hand. Breathe into your lower dantien, and focus on the healing energy and vibrational nourishment you have cultivated, penetrating deep into your belly. Stay there as long as you would like, savoring the energy in your lower dantien and enjoying the vibrational nourishment you have cultivated.

To get the most out of this practice, it is important to visualize the energy. Use your imagination to create greater awareness of the energy you are cultivating. If you go through the motions in a mechanical way, it will not have the same healing effect. Stay at the lower dantien, with all this cultivated energy, as long as you would like.

The three dantien energy centers from the Taoist system are similar yet different from the yogic system of the chakras. They work together. The chakra system is a vortex of input/output energy for processing and maturing your psyche. The dantien centers are for storing life force energy or chi, as explained above. Both are important for enlivening your body and illuminating your soul.

The lower dantien is also referred to as the spiritual embryo. It is an energy center, or elixir field; it is your power center. You have a lower dantien, which is the one I've referred to. You also have a middle dantien and an upper dantien. The middle dantien is in the area of your heart, and the upper dantien is your third eye or intuitive center. When I heard about the lower dantien being the spiritual embryo, I realized my belly held something special and should always be honored. I have since taken on a sense of wonderment, knowing my lower belly is a place where my spirituality is birthed. Now I put my hand over my dantien and question, how can I illuminate and awaken my spirit in my body even more? Inside me lies this embryo wanting to be birthed. I now have reverence and respect for my lower belly, because I know it holds something very special.

EXERCISE: FILLING YOUR SENSUAL HOLE

Here, I will present an excellent vibrational nourishment exercise to "fill your hole," especially when you are single or are not receiving outside sensual stimulation such as sexual contact or even cuddling. Cuddling releases oxytocin, a brain chemical that creates nurturing and connection. It is a love potion built right into your body. It has been shown to induce optimism, reduce stress and relieve pain when produced in the body. Oxytocin is released by a mother right after giving birth; it is activated by her newborn suckling her breasts. It is the connection and bonding chemical. It is a wonderful chemical for the body to feel love, trust and nourishment. Your skin is your largest organ. Simply by touching your skin, you will increase your oxytocin levels.

To fill your sensual hole, lie naked on a big soft blanket while playing some sensual music. Find the most luxurious, luscious, soft and cushy blanket you have, or buy one. Lie down and roll around, letting all your body parts come in contact with the soft sensual touch of the blanket. Let your body explore various movements as you roll around, twisting and turning. Sensually touch those parts of your body not in contact with the soft, cushy blanket. Feel the softness of the blanket on your skin, and feel the touch of your hands on your skin. Let the music inspire you to new sensual heights as you cultivate vibrational nourishment in your body.

Take extra time to explore and touch your face sensually with your fingertips. Touch your lips. They have many nerve endings. Be present; feel the full sensation of the moment as your fingertips caress and explore your face sensually. Allow yourself to indulge in the experience of self-induced sensual delight. This practice helps you cultivate sensual self-love. It is a simple practice and doesn't have to take long, but energetically it has a long-lasting effect of creating vibrational nourishment in your body. This practice prevents you from being susceptible to having sensual or sexual experiences that are not in your best interest.

EXERCISE: BREAST MASSAGE

Another vibrational nourishment exercise is breast massage. Our breasts are our love pillows. Our breasts represent mothering, nurturing and nourishment. Our breasts and our hearts are our Love Center. Massaging your breasts is an important part of a woman's health. However, most women don't know this. Culturally, it is not something women talk about, let alone do as a normal practice. However, this is something every woman should know about. Breast massage is a beautiful way for a woman to send inward what she so naturally gives to others: her loving, nurturing energy.

Massaging your breasts is simple and pleasurable. It helps prevent cancer, as well as detect it. It helps keep breast skin supple and adds resiliency to breast tissue. It is a way to be intimate with your breasts and cultivate self-nourishment. The importance of breast massage is a missing piece of women's wisdom in our culture.

Breast massage enhances lymphatic flow. The lymphatic system has no pump, as does the circulatory system (the heart is its pump). Massaging the breasts increases lymphatic flow. The lymphatic system works in concert with your immune system and your emotions. Your immune system and emotions hold the secret to your longevity. Breast massage stimulates the immune system and nurtures your emotions. The thymus gland, which is the master gland of the immune system, is located right above the heart and is touched and positively affected when you massage your breasts.

In addition, breast self-massage is safe and, like few things in life, free. With all these benefits, why not incorporate this into your life as a woman?

The medical community encourages us to have mammograms. The process may be useful for early detection of breast cancer; however, I believe breasts would rather be massaged instead of radiated, analyzed, pinched or prodded. I believe all they need is love.

When you visit a gynecologist, they ask if you do regular breast exams and they give you a handout describing how to do it. I think that is fine, AND at the same time, I don't agree fully with the methodology. When you do a breast exam, you are looking for something that is *wrong*. The mind wants to find something that isn't supposed to be there. The intention is to look for something defective or wrong. I would rather look for something that is *right*. A more positive approach is regular breast massage and feeling all that is right, not wrong, with your breasts. If you practice regular breast self-massage, you will notice if something has changed. The difference is that you won't be specifically looking for it. Seek and ye shall find. If you seek tumors, you will find them. If you seek health and wellness, you will find it. What do you want to look for?

Breast problems such as cysts, lumps and soreness are a result of accumulated energy in the breasts. If done regularly, breast self-massage will facilitate release of this energy to free you of these problems.

Women who go braless have a reduced risk of breast cancer by a factor of twenty. Bras with an elastic strap, or worse, an underwire, hinder immune response, slow lymph fluid circulation and trap energy in the breasts. If you have to wear a bra, take time when you are at home to be bra-less. It is good for your health. By not wearing a bra, you are giving yourself some vibrational nourishment.

The nipples are related to the endocrine system. When you massage your nipples, you can actually affect your endocrine system and hormones in a positive way. The tissue of the breasts is related to your organs, and massaging your breast tissue can affect your organs in a positive way. The breasts are directly connected to the ovaries and uterus, therefore nurturing massage to your breasts also enhances and sends positive energy to your ovaries and uterus. Your nipples also energetically absorb things from the environment. Massaging your nipples allows you to clear this energy and release toxic buildup.

When you massage your breasts, you are filling your breast tissue with life force energy. You are filling them up. Energetically, your breasts are getting bigger. With a dedicated practice of breast self-massage, women have actually experienced physical enlargement of their breasts. Either way, energetically they are getting bigger. You are filling your whole chest area with nurturing and healing energy, which in turn helps open your heart. The nurturing, healing love energy you cultivate when you massage your breasts is sent inward instead of outward. You are converting your sexual energy into compassion, renewal and revitalization. You are creating vibrational nourishment in your chest, heart, lungs and breasts.

When you massage your breasts, you can do it with clothes on or without. You can use massage oil or not. The main thing is to do it, and do it regularly. It takes time, dedication and commitment. I am not perfect at doing breast massage regularly, however I do it as often as I can, and it is a big part of how I have enhanced my relationship with my body.

Gentle breast massage with oil will relieve premenstrual tender nipples and clear stagnant energy that is causing the tenderness. Do it very gently, bringing healing life force energy into the breasts, heart and chest area.

I owe the transformation of my relationship with my breasts to Saida Desilets, PhD. She was one of my teachers when I received my certification as a Spiritual Sexual Educator with the Divine Feminine Institute. She is doing powerful work in the world helping women reclaim their erotic innocence. She is the author of *Emergence of the Sensual Woman*. Her book has been a great resource for me since I graduated from the program. The techniques I will discuss are techniques she showed us in class and that I have used ever since. I will summarize the techniques. If you want a more detailed Taoist meaning of the techniques as related to the organs, you can purchase her book. She has detailed information and wonderful sensual practices.

Saida Desilets is a global thought leader in women's psychosexual health. She is dedicated to inspiring women to claim and live by their own sexual sovereignty. I am thankful she came into my life.

Breast Massage Technique

When doing breast massage, take enough time for yourself so you can enjoy the experience without distractions. Rub your hands together to create energy in your hands before you do each of the following breast massage techniques. Inhale, and then as you exhale, place your hands on your breasts, and tune into the feeling of energy and vibrational nourishment penetrating into your breasts. Allow yourself to receive the healing, nurturing, loving energy you are directing into your breasts from your hands.

Below are some different techniques. See you if you come up with others as well.

Breast Massage Methods

Nipples – After rubbing your hands together and inhaling, place the palms of your hands over your nipples. Then tune in and experience your breasts receiving the warm healing energy coming into your nipples.

Breast Tissue – Place your hands on your breast tissue. Feel the warmth of your hands penetrating deep into your breast tissue. Begin to circle your hands either in an inward rotation or in an outward rotation around the nipples. Move slowly and feel the warmth of your hands penetrating into your breasts. The outward circles are for clearing, and the inward circles are for cultivating. Do the outward circles first to clear, followed by the inward circles to cultivate. The outward circles are generally related to decreasing the size of the breasts, and the inward circles are generally related to increasing the size of the breasts. Take your time and be present with your touch. There is no guarantee that with this technique you can increase your breast size if you so desire, however with regular dedicated practice it has been known to happen.

Squeeze Breast Tissue – Squeezing the breast tissue also helps release stagnant energy in the breasts. Place your hands on the outer base of each breast and squeeze the tissue as you move in the direction of the nipples. As you squeeze the tissue and move toward the nipples, continue the movement as if you are taking energy out of your breast tissue through your nipples and releasing it out of the body. Do this with intention for however many cycles you feel are right.

Press and Release – This exercise stimulates the thymus (the master gland of the immune system). Remember, the immune system works in concert with your emotions and the lymphatic system. Place your hands on the lower outside area of your breasts. Press your breast tissue up and inward toward the center of your chest, then release the pressure, releasing your hands from having contact with your breasts (about an inch away). Let the breasts fall back into place. You will experience a feeling of release or energy move through the center of your chest. This brings energy into your thymus gland as well as moving nourishing energy through your breast tissue.

EXERCISE: THE ROYAL EGG

The last vibrational nourishment practice I want to discuss is the Royal Egg. The custom of wearing a crystal egg in your vagina comes from Ancient China. It was a secret practice reserved for women in the royal palaces. It is said that this practice will keep a woman's sexual organs as succulent and resilient as that of a young woman, for her entire life. This wisdom, this ancient knowledge, is now available to you.

It is common for women to suffer from female reproductive ailments at some point in their lives, and for some it is chronic. Many women go to the gynecologist because of chronic urinary tract or yeast infections. Many women also suffer from a loss of bladder control due to weak pelvic floor muscles. This condition is common among women of all age groups, not just women who have given birth, although that is a common cause. Many women believe this is a natural part of aging. Our pelvic floor muscles start to atrophy when we are young, but it is not because we have or haven't given birth. It happens because we don't generally exercise these muscles. The Royal Egg provides a way to exercise these muscles and bring vibrational nourishment to your female anatomy.

Pelvic floor muscles support your reproductive organs and other vital organs. Over time, if these muscles are not kept toned, your organs will drop. This can cause lower back pain and discomfort, which could also be experienced during intercourse. The weakening of the pelvic floor muscles also causes a weakening of a woman's pleasure, since her orgasmic contractions would be weaker. Wearing the Royal Egg provides vibrational nourishment for the pelvic region and female anatomy. It also provides ongoing "female fitness," automatically working the pelvic floor muscles by keeping the egg in place.

The egg facilitates getting to know the bottom of your body in a new way. It cultivates and refines your sexual energy. Using the egg assists in clearing the Yoni. The traditional practice from the lineage of female Taoists is to use a jade egg. Saida Desilets introduced me to the jade egg practices. The jade egg practices in her book are her distillation of key pieces of wisdom that have been passed to her by various teachers, her own experiences and inner guidance. There is also the rose quartz egg. Saida recommends not using a rose quartz egg unless you feel your Yoni is energetically clear to prevent from growing negative energy patterns. Rose quartz has the frequency of love; therefore, it is a powerful crystal. Though Saida recommends not using a rose quartz egg initially, I have not found it to be a problem for women.

What I share with you below is my own method of working with the egg, and how I have, with this practice, created vibrational nourishment in my Yoni and my whole being.

A beautiful way to incorporate the egg into your life is by wearing it during yoga. If you have a yoga practice, you may be familiar with Mula Bhanda. This is one of three body locks that allows you to hold your energy in instead of losing it. It prevents leakage of vital life force and sexual energy. Wearing the egg while you practice yoga is a perfect way to strengthen your pelvic floor muscles. As you practice yoga and do your Mula Bhanda, you will contract your muscles with extra weight resistance, toning your pelvic floor muscles even more. It is similar to when people put ankle or wrist weights on and do exercises. It adds extra weight-training value. Also, the stretching and deep breathing during yoga, along with the egg as extra resistance, helps enhance the elevation of your spiritual energy. It lifts your sexual energy inward and upward, transforming it into higher spiritual energy instead of leaking out or being stuck in the lower centers of the body. If you have a yoga practice, make it a habit to wear your egg when you go to yoga. You will get the extra benefit of working your Mula Bhanda and working your Kundalini pump, your spiritual pump, to awaken your human potential and send vibrational nourishment up your spine.

If you use the egg with intention, it can penetrate, purify and transform the core of your being. We have been letting men penetrate the core of our being, and all too often without much consciousness. My wish for you is that your Royal Egg becomes your guiding friend to create greater awareness and deeper discovery of your feminine essence. The deeper discovery I am talking about is a subtle energy that can be missed if you don't give yourself the time and commitment necessary for its discovery and development. Letting yourself slow down and "smell the roses" is a crucial part of this journey.

If you do nothing but wear your Royal Egg on a regular basis, you will enhance the health and vitality of your pelvic floor and female anatomy. Let your Royal Egg help you explore and discover the feminine mystery of self-empowerment. Life doesn't have to be so emotional. Life doesn't have to be so hard. This precious little egg doesn't have all the answers. However, it may help heal the deepest part of you and awaken your inner beauty. This egg can, and will, literally lift your feminine self-esteem.

Eckhart Tolle, in his bestselling book, *A New Earth*, writes about the flowering of human consciousness. As I read that, I could only think about how it is related to women and the feminine mysteries we hold. Unfortunately, these are still almost complete mysteries to many women. As we develop our feminine strength and feminine confidence and express it in our intimate relationships, we create a change on a micro level that has a ripple effect on the macro level, which is actually the process of ushering in a better world.

"All this responsibility between our legs?" you ask. Well, if we are really going to get to the "core" of what is happening in our society and invoke change, then the answer may well be, "Yes."

Through the process of working with the egg, you will bring more awareness to those parts of you that need your attention, acceptance and love. If not attended to, these areas can, and will, ultimately bring you ill health, physically, emotionally or spiritually. The egg, when worn with intention, can be a powerful tool for women to keep their spirits bright. At times, we are baffled by our own behavior and how emotional we can get. I believe we, the feminine, the receptive, the inney—take on other people's energy far easier than men do. It is important for women to be aware of this.

Our vaginas are open tubes of receptivity. What energies are you receiving? How can you better manage those energies and not take on negative energies? Most women don't give their female anatomy much spiritual attention. Giving your female anatomy spiritual attention by changing how you perceive it will create greater awareness, brightness and healing. Wearing your Royal Egg provides the much-needed spiritual attention and vibrational nourishment your Yoni longs for.

Let your egg be your friend of positive intention in conjunction with your imagination. Always put your egg in with a blessing or intention, and let the egg shine that blessing within you as you wear it. It doesn't have to take long to do so. There is a divine energy running through time and space to nourish us, and all we have to do is tap into it. I am sure you have felt this energy when you pray, or when you are in a positive state of mind. We are connected to this energy. Your egg can help you draw on this energy to create vibrational nourishment in the root of your being.

We are constantly exposed to energies we cannot see, yet they can profoundly affect our state of mind and our health, especially with women, since we are the inneys. Here are some examples of how you can use intention, invocation and imagination to put your Royal Egg to work for you.

1. It keeps your sexual organs cleansed on a spiritual level. Women are receptive. We can take on energy during sexual intercourse and literally lose ourselves. You can energetically rebalance yourself using the healing properties of your egg.
2. The egg will help when you go into a meeting, appointment or discussion where you know your energy is going to be pulled down. Wear the egg, and imagine it shining brightly when the discussion gets difficult.
3. It will help when you go somewhere where the energy is too much for you. Imagine the egg in you radiating out powerful beams of protective energy as you walk through the crowd or are in the presence of people.
4. It will help you feel protected when you go on a trip by yourself and want to be safe. Imagine the egg inside you with rays of protective energy around you at all times.
5. Put the egg in for healing and imagine its brightness shining throughout the day.
6. If you carry shame in your Yoni, ask for healing. Wear your egg, and then when you remove it, visualize the shame being released from your body.
7. If you are single, imagine your egg attracting your perfect partner.
8. If you are a healer, massage therapist or counselor, you can wear the egg with the intention of not taking on your client's energy during the session.

Invocations or setting intentions in this sacred way is the process of manifesting the support of that spiritual essence, bringing it into your everyday life and creating a better reality for yourself. It is our responsibility to hold this spiritual essence in our hearts (and Yonis), and carry it forth from generation to generation, to assist in creating ever more light in our bodies. These intentions or prayers work best when you are clear and passionate about what you want. At the same time, let go of any attachment to the outcome.

In additional to placing your egg inside you with intention, I suggest you learn how to sip your egg in as well. Place the larger side of the egg at the opening to your vagina. Push it slightly into the opening of your vagina and by contracting your muscles, you can "sip" the egg into your vagina. It takes a level of Yoni muscular control to do this, which enhances your relationship with your female anatomy.

Your egg symbolizes the inner part of you that is coming out into the world. As you bring your egg in and out of your vagina, you create a connection to the divine feminine within you. You cultivate vibrational nourishment, and your female anatomy is no longer a stranger.

If you don't have a Royal Egg, you can purchase one on my website at www.Anna-Thea.com. Please make sure you read the instructions before using it.

Let these vibrational nourishment practices be part of your life. Make nurturing and supporting your feminine essence important. Let your sensual side express itself in a way that is expansive and enlivening.

EXERCISE:

In this chapter, we explored many ways to have a love affair with your body. What resonated most with you? What practices and/or principles can you implement starting TODAY? Below, list five things you are willing to do to cultivate a love affair with your body.

1.____

2.____

3.____

4.____

5.____

CHAPTER 5

Putting More Love Into Your Sexuality

Love your body... Every single part
Especially your Yoni
Now is the time to start

Your "Sacred Space"
Is calling you
To expand and express
Wanting a hug from you

Keep her warm... safe and sound
Let her sing in a way
That is profound

One of wisdom, authentic pleasure
And knowing what is right
No longer having to fake or put up a fight

Love your body... Every single part
Especially your Yoni
Now is the time to start

In the previous chapter, we discussed many ways to listen, enliven and illuminate your body. We covered ways to deal with intense emotions and introduced vibrational nourishment practices for your feminine soul. In this last chapter, we will talk about your sacred sexuality. We will cover how putting love into your sexuality will not only empower you, but will also bless the world with your divine feminine essence.

MANIFESTING MORE PLEASURE IN YOUR LIFE

Do you want to experience more pleasure in your life and body? If that is what you would like, it begins with you. You can't look outside yourself to create it; you will always come up short. As the cigarette ad said, "You've Come a Long Way, Baby." We still have such a long way to go. If you want to have a pleasurable sex life, you first need to create a pleasurable sex life with yourself. You need to fall head over heels in love with you!

The intimacy you have with yourself is the foundation to creating a better relationship with your lover. The depth of intimacy you have with yourself will attract a partner who can go equally as deeply and intimately.

If the sex life you have with yourself is simply a matter of putting your hand in your crotch or pulling your vibrator out, bringing yourself to orgasm and falling asleep, then you will attract a guy who is going to do the same, a man who has a quick orgasm in you and falls asleep. This is exactly what needs to shift. We are energy. Our sexual behavior with ourselves creates a certain type of energy field around us. It will determine what we attract into our lives.

Whether you are in a love relationship or not, it is important to deepen your relationship with yourself. This includes the sexual, sensual relationship you have with yourself. Don't ask for intimacy with another if you are not willing to be intimate with yourself. The intimacy you have with yourself is the foundation to creating a better relationship with your lover. The depth of intimacy you have with yourself will attract a partner who can go equally as deeply and intimately.

If you want to have a more pleasurable relationship with your body and your sexuality, it is important, as a woman, to cultivate your sexual energy and put love into it. What I am referring to is cultivating YOUR sexual energy, not as defined by anyone else. Your sexuality specifically defined by you. What is your sexuality? What do you need? What do you like? What have you not discovered yet about your body, your Yoni and your sexual response system? Are you worth exploring? Yes, you most certainly are!

The evolution and flowering of the feminine sexual response system supports the evolution of our human consciousness. Through exploring, discovering and awakening our divine feminine and our female anatomy, we will soften into our feminine power instead of having to live like a man in a man's world. First, we need to uncover our individual and unique sexual needs. They have been covered up in this masculine, "go for it," "make it happen" type world. We have had to abandon our true nature of receptivity and become more masculine to survive. That is changing. Are you part of the change?

We are now all, both men and women, being called to soften and awaken our feminine essence to create a more balanced world. Tami Kent, author of *Wild Feminine*, says:

> *The truth is that the feminine has never left us. Women, and men, have abandoned the feminine. We have forgotten what it means to live by our feminine principles. Living in profound disconnect from the earth, in the frantic pace of life unmoved by our own natural inner rhythms that alternate between expansive creation and restorative*

retreat, we have precious little time or space to invite the appearance of the feminine. In fact, we will not encounter the feminine until we return to the place we first met her: the female body.

You might feel confused regarding how to soften and awaken your feminine essence, yet remain empowered. It is because very few people have experienced it. We have been too caught up in a more masculine way of life with its manic pace and disconnect from nature, Mother Earth and her natural rhythms. There is no time to slow down in such a fast-paced world. Luckily for you, as a woman, the fastest way for you to reconnect with your softer side and your femininity is to connect to that which you hold at the bottom of your body, your feminine essence. You as a woman are the embodiment of the feminine essence. When you acknowledge and honor the feminine essence that you hold in the root of your being, this feminine essence will no longer elude you. She is right there inside of you, waiting for you to discover her on a deeper level. Your feminine essence needs your presence, reverence and unconditional love. Are you willing to give her that?

PLEASURE AND RECEPTIVITY

Many women in our society carry sexual wounds. If you have been sexually abused, you have wounds in your body from those experiences. Even if you weren't sexually abused, the collective consciousness of the world is such that it has wounded most everyone's sexuality. Men, too, have been sexually wounded. If you want to love your body and feel empowered in it, you need to look at your sexuality...heal, awaken, expand and put more love into it.

In *A New Earth*, Eckhart Tolle speaks of "the pain body," a residue of past emotionally painful experiences stored in the cells of the body. What women need to know is that there is a magnificent, marvelous and mysterious counterpart to that, "the pleasure body." The female body is designed for tremendous sensual pleasure, and the female brain is wired to give us an opportunity for the full experience of those pleasures.

We are the leaders of love. The masculine way to lead is through conquering. The feminine way is through intuition and surrendering to our innate desire to lead with love and feel great sensual pleasure in our bodies. Feeling pleasure is how we let love in so we can lead with love. The more we calm our busy minds, the greater the opportunity to experience deep love, acceptance and more pleasure in our bodies. If you have had body image issues, you hold pain in your body. It is time to let that pain go. Allow pleasure in. Opening up your body and letting pleasure in heals body image issues. When you let love and pleasure into your body, you stop the internal battle you may be experiencing.

As women, we have not been programmed to open up to, and accept, delight and bodily pleasure. Historically, we haven't had a safe space for such receptivity. It takes effort to change our attitude and programming about pleasure. Pain may motivate, because we want to avoid it, but pleasure heals. When you take time and learn how to open deeper into pleasure, you will heal the relationship you have with your body.

Your ability to feel pleasure is related to your ability to *open* and *receive.* We live in a world where the natural tendency is to react by shutting down instead of staying open or opening up. In new situations, we tend to be suspicious, defensive or judgmental. It takes effort and consciousness to keep ourselves open. That is why for many, pleasure is elusive. I am not only referring to sexual pleasure or our bodies. In general, we are not raised to be receptive.

For example, what happens when someone gives a woman a compliment on her pretty dress? How often does the woman reply, "Oh, there's a hole or a snag here at the bottom," instead of staying open, receptive and truly receiving the compliment? Somehow, it is automatic to find fault and not fully receive the compliment, smile and say thank you. The next time someone compliments you, notice your response. See if you can stay open and receive the compliment without resistance. See if you can receive the compliment without acting on an impulse to return the compliment. See if you can simply receive.

To become more receptive and create more pleasure in your life, you need to be able to ask for what you need, create a deeper understanding of your feminine parts, and create safe situations so your body will respond and open.

All of this requires learning the language of needs and feelings. If you are not connected to your feelings and unmet needs, they stay bottled up and will remain stuck in your body. No wonder the "natural" response is to shut down. Women must feel and understand their needs and be able to ask for what they need. You have to learn how to feel and be present with your uncomfortable feelings. You must recognize, acknowledge and experience them instead of stuffing them, if you are going to get to the good feelings and create satisfying intimate relationships in your life. Most of us need help to learn the language of needs and feelings. I definitely needed support and guidance as I learned this new and empowering language. My coaching program addresses these issues, and gives you the support and tools to navigate uncomfortable feelings, instead of numbing them, so you can be a sensually alive woman.

To cultivate receptivity it is also important to create a safe space. When you are relaxed, you feel safe. How can you open and receive when you are in fight or flight mode, stressed out or filled with anxiety? In order to open and receive, create safe spaces for yourself. If you are by yourself and do vibrational nourishment exercises, make sure to do them when you have enough time and won't be interrupted. If you are being intimate with someone, make sure it is in a setting where you feel comfortable and uninhibited. Choose to be intimate with someone who is also safe to be with, someone who values your needs and is attentive. There is nothing worse for a woman's receptivity than a selfish lover. Women are starving for conscious touch. Through conscious touch, we will awaken the deeper parts of our female sexual response system and feminine power.

CONSCIOUS TOUCH

Through conscious touch, we can use our sexual energy as a healing force. It is the path for us to become each other's healers instead of a source of each other's wounds. Sexual energy is mysterious and powerful. On a physical level, it is powerful enough to ensure our existence as a species. On a refined level, it awakens us to our power, our eternal essence, and it allows us to see who we are beyond our bodies and to embrace the brilliance of our soul. Ultimately, it connects us to Spirit.

Awakening the divine feminine within through conscious touch is a beautiful way to refine your raw sexual energy. It is about awakening to the present moment and experiencing its richness and fullness. When we spend most of our time in our heads, it is a challenge to drop down into the present moment. When you are goal-oriented in your sexual expression, you can easily miss the bliss. It will always be just outside your reach.

Don't miss the bliss! Your *body* is always in the present moment. Conscious touch drops you into your body and frees you from the incessant mind chatter that keeps you from pleasure.

When you are goal-oriented in your sexual expression, you can easily miss the bliss. It will always be just outside your reach. Don't miss the bliss!

What is conscious touch? We live in a touch-deprived world. We all can learn to touch each other more consciously. Through conscious touch, we can heal relationships. Conscious touch is the path to becoming a heart-centered master of your sexual energy.

ELEMENTS OF CONSCIOUS TOUCH:

- Conscious touch is to touch another without an agenda, without wanting to manipulate, control or have a specific outcome.
- Conscious touch takes place when you touch another after first asking permission. Often we think our partner's body is our body, but it isn't. It is theirs. Asking permission creates reverence and respect.
- Conscious touch occurs when you are centered in your body and connected to your breath, and you understand that your hands are an extension of your heart. It is the ability to send heart energy and love from your heart, through your arms to the receiver.
- Conscious touch happens when you are able to create a safe space for the receiver to open up and receive in a way that allows that person to connect more deeply to him or herself.

All too often, we touch another or receive touch when we are under stress, transmitting stress energy. Or we touch as a way to reach a goal instead of simply being present and giving love. Our hands are transmitters of love. Remember the acronym HANDS – Heal, Awaken and Nurture, Doing it Sensually. Awaken your healing hands, and let them transform your sexual life.

TALK ABOUT SEX / SHIFT ATTTITUDES

Talk about sex as if it is a fascinating subject, because it is. Talk it up! Celebrate it. Sharing our most intimate experiences with others is not something we do regularly in our culture. We save that for counseling sessions, and then we talk about it as a problem. Sharing with each other what we have experienced, as long as it respects all people involved, is a way of learning from each other. Keeping our sexual experiences to ourselves and hidden can lead to unnecessary suffering. People can have questions, concerns, doubts and even negative ideas about their sexuality because they don't know that what they are experiencing is normal and natural. There is no need to suffer when it comes to your sexuality, your creative life force energy. How can we shift our attitudes about sexuality so there is less suffering and more celebration?

If we don't talk about sex openly and freely, even with gusto and excitement, then we will continue to live in the Dark Ages. Sex put us here, and we joke about it, have shame hangovers about it, commit rape and repress that which is our creative life force. Our sexual energy, how we move around in it, how we share it and how we focus its energy, is a reflection of who we are. Your sexual relationship with yourself or with another is a glimpse or reflection of who you are and how the relationship is overall.

Much can be healed by shifting our attitudes about sex. Our self-esteem, our relationship with our bodies, our interactions with others and our attitudes about the opposite sex will benefit when we change our attitudes about sex. We were born into a world that has some turned-around sexual attitudes. While we are gaining more awareness about the sacredness of sexuality, we are still in the process of freeing ourselves of the Puritan influences which made sex sinful, secretive, and most of all—disempowering to women. Tantric, or Sacred Sexual, teachings from reputable leaders can help you release deep programming of dysfunctional relating, limiting beliefs and sexual shame. It can also help you establish more reverence for the power you hold as a sexual being, and for sexual union.

What words do *you* use when talking about sex? Language is powerful and shapes our reality. The palate, or meridian points, at the roof of our mouth could be referred to as a computer keyboard to our consciousness. When we speak, our tongues strike different areas of our mouths. This sends signals or vibrations to the higher centers in our brain and influences our consciousness.

Let's look at the words commonly used when talking about sex, this most amazing and noble force that can create another human. The words aren't indicative of such a noble power. For a man's penis, there is cock, rod or even sword. For a woman's genitals, there is snatch, bush and more. For the sexual act, we have called it getting laid or getting off. The "F" word is associated with sexual union, but it is also something you say when you are enraged with someone. When someone says "F--- You" loudly and with intense emotional pain, it is actually a cry for connection. In the moment of that outburst, they are shielding their precious vulnerable heart.

On the Oxford Dictionaries website, the first definition of the "F" word is, "to have sexual intercourse (with someone)." That's the official and primary meaning of the word. It also defines a secondary meaning, "to ruin or damage (something)." How did sexual union, for some, become associated with being ruined or damaged?

The Ancient Tantric traditions are a form of spiritual sexuality. Tantric traditions use terminology that invokes a sense of sacredness to describe our sexual body parts. The words we choose to describe our sexual body parts reflect how we think about them. For the man's sexual body part, instead of being a cock or rod or other slang descriptors, Tantric traditions refer to a man's penis as a Lingam. Lingam translated means *Wand of Light*. We want our men to have a wand of light, a magical mystical healing device. Instead, in our history, it has been a sword that rapes, pillages, impregnates and abandons. Obviously not all men have done this. There are many good men, and we are more civilized now than we were in the past. Nonetheless, our history holds violence and horrendous human atrocities, many of which were inflicted upon women. I believe the energy of these trespasses is still present in the cellular memory of women's bodies. A woman referring to her man's genitalia as a wand of light energetically helps to clear these memories and encourages him to use it as such.

As I mentioned earlier, a woman's female genitalia is called a Yoni, which means Sacred Space. Referring to your female genitalia as a Yoni is a powerful way to empower you and your feminine parts. Yoni is a beautiful word, and can be used in normal social situations. You can't as easily, in a social conversation, say pussy or beaver. When you do, it sounds derogatory. Using the word Yoni brings a sense of loveliness to that area of a woman's body, both for those who use the word and those who hear it. I encourage you to, if you don't already, refer to your feminine parts as Yoni unless you have some other word that is of equal elegance.

Another Tantric term is Amrita. Amrita translated means *divine nectar*. The ejaculatory fluid that we as women release is sacred fluid. All of our sexual body fluids, both men's and women's, are sacred and are not something to be repulsed by. I talk more about Amrita in the section of this chapter entitled, "Knowing What's Down There."

I have always found the subject of sex fascinating. I always wanted to talk about it and hear different people's perspectives about it. I felt this was how I could learn and have a better understanding of my own sexuality, human behavior and the full meaning of sexual interactions. I always felt fascinated by this powerful energy, our sexuality, and how we express it. I knew it contained tremendous power. As I learned later, it holds the blueprint of our human potential.

KUNDALINI

Kundalini energy is a spiritual energy. It is a female energy sleeping in the sexual region of our bodies, often stuck in the lower three chakras, keeping us disempowered and unaware. It is up to each individual to awaken it. It is your raw sexual energy, also referred to as Shakti. It is an inner fire with tremendous force and potential. This powerful feminine force has the ability to either bind or liberate you; it is your choice. Shiva is Shakti's male counterpart.

Shiva (the masculine principle) represents all consciousness and Shakti (the feminine principle) is the agent of change to make things manifest, not only in the universe as a whole but in each individual. Shiva is the "God" and Shakti the "Goddess." Shiva represents Source and Shakti represents the creation of that source energy. In a sense they are one and the same. Shiva is changelessness and Shakti is change. The feminine principles, Shakti and Kundalini, are responsible for creation and are the agents of all change.

Kundalini is described as a sleeping three-coiled serpent at the base of your spine. As long as this energy remains asleep, the individual soul is limited in his or her awareness. It is also referred to as the Holy Spirit. This energy, when released from the base of the spine, moves upwards through the spine and the chakra systems. It clears blocks and will free us from dysfunctional ways of living and relating.

The spine is the electrical circuit for your aliveness. The body contains many energy channels called *nadis*. These are energy channels that, when awakened, connect us to more subtle spiritual energies in our body. According to Ayurveda (India's traditional system of medicine, more than five thousand years old, which uses diet, herbal treatment and yogic breathing to support health), the body has 72,000 nadis. These nadis radiate out from our chakras and communicate with all parts of the body. We are a stream of energy channels wanting to be opened! The three main nadis run up and down the spine. They are called the Ida, Pingala and Sushumna. The Ida and Pingali wrap around the spine and the chakras. The Ida nadi is the feminine channel in your body, and the Pingali is the masculine channel in your body. Balanced energy flow between these two nadis creates balance in your life. The Sushumna is in the center of the spine and is the channel through which the Kundalini, our spiritual energy, rises through the body.

Kundalini represents the reservoir of power within us; a tremendous volume of pure passion, drive and desire.

Kundalini can be awakened through breath, movement and sound. Kundalini yoga is a form of yoga that works with these three principles, incorporating physical exercises, breath, chants and music to help accomplish this awakening. Because it is the technology of awareness, I believe Kundalini yoga helps refine and spiritualize your sexual energy.

When the Kundalini begins to rise through the central channel of your spine and move through the chakras, unresolved issues stuck in any of the chakras will surface. Just as our emotions tend to stir things up, Kundalini moves up the spine and through the chakras, stirring up, waking up and opening any blocks that are ready to be released. Kundalini represents the reservoir of power within us; a tremendous volume of pure passion, drive and desire. As our Kundalini moves up the spine, she undulates, similar to that of a snake slithering across the ground or a woman dancing. In religious traditions, this coiled serpent, this feminine energy, Kundalini, has been depicted as evil or dangerous. It is *not* dangerous, but rather a threat to those who want to keep individuals down and unaware of their own power so they can be controlled.

In summary, Kundalini, feminine energy, when fully awakened, is how we free ourselves from the restrictions of the physical world and create a more pleasurable life. It is how we illuminate and activate our radiant bodies. It is the birthing of the divine feminine within us. Kundalini allows us to reclaim the sacredness of our bodies and feel empowered. It is the process of opening to the subtle energy that allows us to be in our bodies at a higher vibration or consciousness.

Tantra, or Sacred Sexuality, works with the Kundalini energy and with the weaving of masculine and feminine energies to find balance. It is about honoring both the male and female energies, and understanding that one cannot exist without the other. They are interdependent and part of the whole. Bringing these energies into balance through awareness and compassion for the differences allows us to celebrate each of their unique qualities. This gives us a path for making masculinity and femininity complimentary instead of opposing. Spiritualizing your sexuality by moving it into the heart allows the two energies of the masculine and feminine to live in harmony.

TANTRA / SPIRITUAL SEXUAL EDUCATION

What is Tantra? The word Tantra has been misused, and possibly even misunderstood in the Western world. It is often associated with having "mind-blowing" sex. It is so much more than that. Tantra is described as powerful celebratory and sacred acts of body, speech and mind. They are practices to awaken and liberate us in our body. These practices can be done individually, with another or in a group (Tantra encompasses non-sexual, clothes-on practices as well). I refer to what I teach as Spiritual Sexual education.

Spiritual Sexual education and putting heart energy into your sexuality helps heal sexual shame and the gap between the sexes. When we heal our relationships, we heal the planet and ourselves. In relationships, there is opportunity for misunderstanding. It is easy to think that the opposite sex is just that, opposite. Spiritual Sexual education supports a shift in perception, where we realize that we don't oppose each other. Men and women were not meant to be opposite; they were magically designed to be complimentary. Our sexuality is a powerful tool for that purpose.

Spiritual Sexual education and putting heart energy into your sexuality will cure, in both sexes, what I refer to as HGS. For men, it stands for "Horny Guy Syndrome." This is what happens when a man focuses his sexual energy primarily on his genitals. His goal becomes release, in whatever form he can achieve it, and not on connection. HGS obscures his ability to have authentic connections. If his unconscious "release" ends up inside a woman, he is dumping his "stuff" into her. She, often unknowingly, becomes a dumping ground for all of his pent-up, unprocessed emotions. His sexual energy is expressed through his groin only instead of also through his heart.

Yonis are wise. Even if the woman doesn't realize it, her Yoni does. Her

Yoni will armor itself up for protection. The woman then becomes inflicted with HGS as well. HGS in women stands for "Hardened Girl Syndrome." Her Yoni and her body know, even if she may not, that her sacred space is being violated and used. A Yoni has a heart meter, and can sense when heart energy is not present in a sexual act. The sex act may even become a commodity where the man develops a sense of entitlement. She may even fall into an obligatory role to satisfy his needs. These are very unhappy Yonis indeed and there are plenty of them on the planet today. The woman has to wall off to keep her vulnerable-self safe. She builds energetic walls and becomes hardened because her Yoni and true feminine are not receiving what they really need, a conscious, present lover. The Yoni and the true feminine want to be honored and revered. Spiritual Sexuality teaches men about emotional availability and being present. It helps men move away from goal-oriented and release-oriented sexual expression. Often, in Tantra workshops, most of the men are older. Not always, but often. These men have moved their mindsets from procreation to vitality and liberation. With youth, both men and women have a strong biologically-based sexual force at work to keep our species alive. As we mature, so does our sexuality.

From an analytical point of view, sex has three major functions: procreation, pleasure and liberation. All three of these components are intertwined in some way. Expressing your sexuality in a more procreative way is primal and is expressed through the lower chakras. Though it can still include pleasure, it is more of an animalistic act. From a biological point of view, it ensures the propagation of our species, and is typically expressed in our younger years.

As you move into midlife, if you want to receive the full benefit of this life-giving energy, it is important to graduate to pleasure as your focus. Some people don't do this. They become sexually shutdown, where all the juice is gone in their relationship. They love and care for each other, but they don't support each other's aliveness. Or they express their sexuality in a repressed way by having affairs. This is common in our culture. It happens, especially in long-term relationships, because of longstanding, unresolved issues and resentments. The relationship becomes a platform of wounding instead of a place for healing. They don't do it on purpose. They simply don't know any other way. It takes energy and effort to shift this pattern. I believe heart-based sexuality is the answer. Through this, we have an opportunity to heal relationships and liberate ourselves.

Heart-based sexuality (Spiritual Sexuality or Tantra) is healing to the body. It is pleasure-based and can make you feel younger. Pleasure can elicit expansiveness in the body. It can support the liberation of your soul. It is a powerful elixir, which is most potent when linked with love. Mixing sexual energy, love and pleasure is a potent force for creating aliveness in the body. It is also a potent force for creating havoc in immature relationships. Navigating sexual energy, love and pleasure for your highest good and the highest good of another is not a simple task. That is why heart-based communication is also vitally important. It creates an emotionally safe space. The better we can communicate, the greater our potential for sexual pleasure.

> ***Moving from a biologically-based sexual expression to a more spiritual and heart-based sexual expression allows us to experience the power and purity of our sexual essence.***

Sexual energy is a powerful force. How can you use this powerful force for liberation? By bringing more love into it and spiritualizing it. Any sexual exchange that creates respect, connection, love and heart expansion is spiritual in nature. Bringing love or heart energy into sex makes sex meaningful instead of meaningless. Doing so allows us to see our sexuality as sacred and share it with a sense of reverence. Embodying your sexuality as sacred can heal pornography addiction, perversions or past sexual abuse.

Moving from a biologically-based sexual expression to a more spiritual and heart-based sexual expression allows us to experience the power and purity of our sexual essence. Having friction sex or sport sex (physical or biologically-based sex or sex purely for self-gratification), though fun, is predominately a physical, biological, procreative act. Nonetheless, in each sex act, there is always something powerfully sacred happening, whether the individuals involved realize it or not. Our sexual energy is our life force energy moving through us. Even when expressed purely on a biological level, the essence of the divine is still present. Spiritually-based sexual practices help us move toward, and expand, our awareness of the divine essence present in any sexual exchange. It allows us to feel our sexual energy through every chakra, not just the lower chakras. It is about moving from the physical to the subtle. In moving to the subtle, we heal sexual shame.

SEXUAL SHAME

Sexual shame is pervasive in our world. It is disempowering to any individual, male or female. You may have had an upbringing such that you don't have a lot of sexual shame. Your parents may have been very open about sexuality. That is wonderful. Regardless of your upbringing, however, in our culture, we all live in a sea of sexual shame. It is all around us. Sexual shame will hold you back from your full potential. It will not allow your sexuality to be expressed in a healthy way, which can affect your health and relationships. Sexual shame can keep you isolated.

When there is sexual shame, it manifests as energy blocks in the body.

By moving your sexual energy in a way that clears the blocks, you can heal sexual shame. Having quick sexual releases, or what I refer to as genital hiccups, can easily keep energy blocked in your genitals. Genitally focused sex and sexual gratification is what I mean by genital hiccups. It doesn't promote heart-centered sexuality. Your sexual expression becomes localized in your groin, limiting the full expression of this life-giving creative force. Instead, allow the sexual energy to move through your whole body, especially through your heart, by delaying gratification. This will allow the sexual energy to be a healing and transformative energy in your body, as well as your psyche.

The heart is the point of entry for sexual connection if we are to heal the wounds between men and women. Teaching men who are sexually attracted to us to "enter" us through our hearts first is of prime importance. It gives a woman a safe space. She will open and become sexually receptive on a deeper level. Sexual expression through the heart becomes wholesome because it moves through the whole body.

When we become more sexually receptive, we become more succulent and vibrant. We no longer have to live a dull sexual life that lacks imagination, feeling and spirit. We are like flowers, and begin to blossom. This is how we learn to love our bodies and become the leaders of love we are meant to be. A woman's path of power is through the path of orgasmic pleasure.

BALANCING THE ORGASM

Healing comes from balancing the feminine and masculine aspects within us. If we are to balance the ratio of orgasms, male to female, I believe women have a lot to catch up on. Women have a lot of pleasure to look forward to if we are to evolve and heal our beautiful planet. This is the birthing of the Divine Feminine.

This is not a burn your bra, feminist movement. We could call it a "Feminine Pleasure Revolution." This is about women getting what they need in order to awaken their sexual response system to its fullest. Men will benefit, because there is nothing more that a man enjoys than a juicy, radiant woman. This is honoring, respecting and giving equal importance to both the masculine and the feminine.

Has a man ever "held space" for your sexuality? Over the course of your sexual history, who has had more orgasms, you or your partner? Have you ever faked an orgasm? Has the sexual act more often been "servicing" him? Holding space for his pleasure? If women are to awaken and be fully empowered in their bodies, it will be through men returning the favor and holding space for us.

What do I mean by holding space for your sexuality? In my training with the Divine Feminine Institute, I learned a form of conscious touch called the nurturing practice of Awakening and Healing (AH), created by Caroline Muir. An AH session can be done fully clothed or completely nude, depending upon your needs and comfort level. The AH practice is a way to hold space for someone's sexuality.

In an AH practice, one person is the receiver and the other is the giver. It is well defined, and there is no confusion. In a typical sex act, this is not the case. Commonly, it becomes a free-for-all, with each person taking turns giving and receiving touch, often frantically moving toward the goal of one or both partners achieving an orgasm. It can get a bit hectic, and even stressful. The individuals may not fully embrace receiving or giving to the depth possible. This prevents both individuals from experiencing full pleasure.

Another common sex act situation is that the couple "has it down," so to speak. They know how to give each other orgasms; therefore, the sex act becomes a utilitarian, non-creative, even non-spiritual expression of "getting each other off." With both sexual expressions, sex often becomes unfulfilling. This is part of the sexual dilemma.

The nurturing practice of AH dissolves this dilemma. In each AH session, there is a giver and receiver as mentioned earlier. The giver is there to "hold space" for the receiver and facilitate an opening to whatever level the receiver is ready to open.

In the illustration (see fig. 11.8), you will see the AH "yoga pose." The receiver is in a reclined position that facilitates an opening. The giver is sitting between the receiver's legs, facing them. The giver has full access to all of the receiver's chakras (energy centers) and body. The AH practice involves eye-gazing, breath, sound, conscious touch and a tremendous amount of presence and intimacy. It is more presence and intimacy than most are accustomed to. That is why the AH practice is transformative. When there is presence, any repressed emotions can easily surface. The giver can simply—with their presence, compassion and love—allow uncomfortable emotions, such as fear, shame, pain and anger to be transformed or released out of the body. This practice helps to bring more aliveness into your body.

The AH practice is a way to hold space for someone's sexuality.

THE AH YOGA POSE

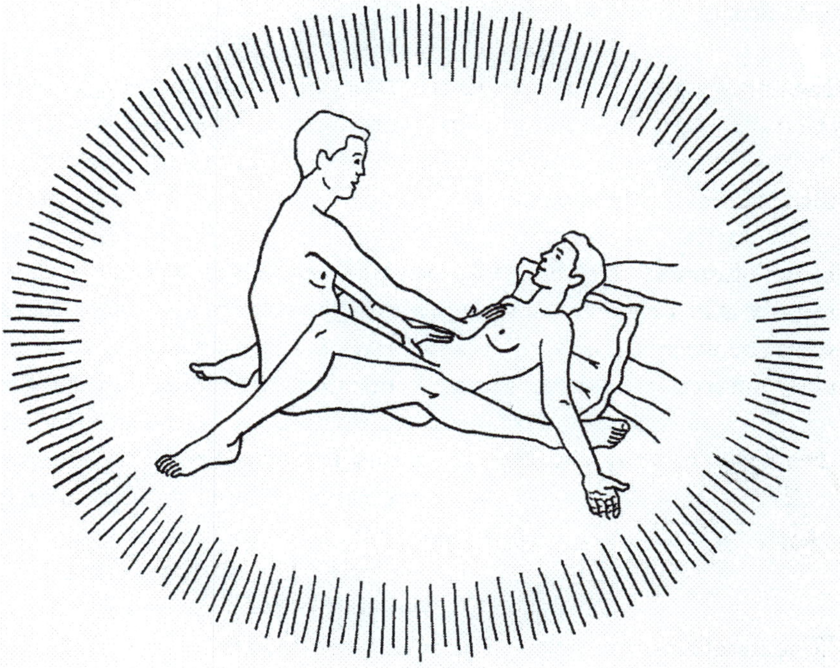

Figure 11.8

During a woman's first AH session, especially if she is not used to receiving, she can experience profound healing. The focus is on the receiver, relaxing her and giving her a safe environment to open up. A woman receiving an AH can access her unlimited, deeply feminine core. It helps her feel more empowered in her body and reinforces her to ask for what she needs. It is a sexual healing practice that supports honoring the body and treating it like a temple.

The sexual healing work (play) you do now will not only heal your current relationships, it will also heal past relationships. It will allow you to see things from a different perspective. As you progress on this path, you will change your current relationships for the better. You may also attract new relationships into your life that are life enhancing instead of life stagnating, or possibly even life threatening.

Most all of us have experienced at least one love relationship that wasn't healthy. Those experiences typically end up being our greatest opportunities for growth. But even in relatively healthy relationships, many women have a difficult time opening to pleasure when engaged in a sexual exchange. Claiming your authentic sexual and sensual self requires you to know your sexual needs. When you do, you will experience more pleasure in your relationship with your body and your sexuality. Creating self-pleasuring sessions with yourself is a good way to "balance the orgasm" because you get to know your sexual needs. I will discuss that shortly, but first I would like to introduce a new word: *outercourse.*

OUTERCOURSE

Sex is generally defined as intercourse. Intercourse itself is commonly not enough to bring a woman to orgasm. As a standard, women's sexual needs aren't met. How can they be met if women don't even know what their needs are? Further, if women have defined any sexual needs, they have often been defined from a masculine perspective.

We have been vulnerable and we have given and allowed entry into our sacred space all too often without question, assuming we were supposed to do so. Many women have intercourse with a man before the third date. We open our vaginas and share our most vulnerable self without question. *I am asking you to question it.* Give yourself time to know more about what type of energy you are allowing inside you before you take in his energy.

Another different perspective would be to give him an opportunity to experience vulnerability before you do. Ask him if he is willing to let you enter him. Men also have a g-spot. The g-spot for a man is also his prostate gland; it is located in a different spot and can be easily accessed through his anus. There is a wide range of perspectives and preferences for men as to whether they will allow themselves to experience the pleasure of their "g-spots." Cultural taboos keep them from engaging in anal entry to access the source of pleasure that is available to them. Heterosexual men may have phobias of being gay if they enjoy such pleasures. This is understandable. Our culture has a strong hold on our belief systems. Nonetheless, the truth is that for men, massaging their prostate gland offers great pleasure. Some men are aware of this, and others aren't. A woman who understands this can ask a man if he would be willing to have her enter him. It requires feminine strength and confidence on a woman's part to offer this. She also has to have a positive attitude about a man's sexuality in order to feel comfortable to give to him in this way.

Why should a woman allow him to enter her if he is not willing to be vulnerable and allow entry as well? You may not find massaging a man's prostrate appealing, and that is fine. However, if you are willing, you offer a way to give a man an opportunity to be vulnerable, too. You support him in opening his receptive channels. You help him tap into his feminine side.

Also, the idea of being called a "tease" will be prevented. Not sharing your sacred space until you are authentically ready to receive is something to honor within yourself. When you receive a man into your sacred space, you take on his psychological imprint for a long time, if not a lifetime. We don't easily rid ourselves of their imprint.

When you ask a man, with all your confidence, if you can enter him, it sheds a new light on the situation. Many men over the centuries haven't asked women. They have taken. By asking men for permission, we can begin to heal that old paradigm where many men chose to take instead of request. What I am suggesting is that when you are in a new and developing love relationship with a man, offer him a prostate massage or something similar to an AH session. Give him an opportunity to show his vulnerability before you so readily open your legs and let him into your sacred well. This takes lots of feminine strength, confidence and sexual consciousness. You are actually offering him a huge blessing by penetrating him with your feminine essence. Are you willing to do this?

With some new relationships, I have had wonderful experiences where intercourse wasn't the emphasis, and the AH practice, sexual healing and outercourse were. It brings a new dynamic into the relationship that is very honoring, freeing and supports the development of intimacy.

Also, this gives you an opportunity to see if a man has some level of mastery with his wand. If he doesn't have mastery and will prematurely ejaculate inside you, I see no reason to have him inside you. Wouldn't you agree? I feel fully comfortable exploring outercourse with a man and holding space for each other's sexual energy until I feel comfortable that I want him inside me. I encourage you to have the feminine strength and confidence to do the same. Otherwise, you could go through a string of men before meeting your mate or compatible companion, and all the while pick up various and sundry men's psychological imprints.

I hear it so often when women talk about someone they are with: "He isn't the right one, but right for now." Having intercourse with someone who isn't the right one and just for now gives your body different signals, especially if you want "the right one" (if there is such a thing). I believe this can short circuit your sexual response system.

Do AH sessions or outercourse instead. AH sessions are wonderful because there is no confusion. They are especially wonderful when you are not quite sure if you are attracted to the person or if you two are a good fit. Use AH to give the relationship time, instead of jumping into a deep connection that confuses the situation and may not work out.

Outercourse and AH practices set the stage for a melting of our hearts, in general terms, a sweet strengthening of women and a gentle softening of men, when we choose to use the nurturing practice of AH and outercourse when beginning a new relationship.

Women typically need more time to respond sexually and often find themselves just warming up and relaxing into the sex act, only to find that their partner is finished. I encourage women to know what they need sexually and to ask for it. Receiving what you need in order to awaken the deeper aspects of your sexual nature has far-reaching implications. Just as we live in a society of fast food diets that provide little nourishment, so too do we live in a world of fast food sex, which leaves us empty, with little nurturing and nourishment.

Women, being the gender that bears children, have an innate ability to nurture and nourish. Therefore, one aspect of balancing our feminine and masculine sexual natures would be to bring in more sexual nurturing. This supports reaching states of ecstatic bliss in an expanded, fulfilling way with no goals, as opposed to one of a more goal-oriented and focused completion of ecstatic release. Integrating outercourse into your sexual life supports the honoring, respecting and giving equal importance to both the masculine and the feminine qualities of our sexual nature. Balancing outercourse with intercourse can help melt the walls that have kept the sexes separate. The nurturing practice of the AH is a form of outercourse that facilitates this. It also helps a woman create more Yoni awareness.

YONI AWARENESS

You create Yoni Awareness when you connect to and honor your female anatomy and divine feminine essence. With Yoni Awareness, you tune into your Yoni; listening to and honoring what she is saying. Many men have been led by their groins, and men themselves have shared this with me. Look at the world. It is not a bad place, but things need improvement. If this world is to become a better, more loving and more conscious place, one of the biggest shifts we need is for women to be led by their Yonis, their true, empowered feminine essence. I believe this is "good medicine" for the world. If we, as women, truly honor our Yonis, what type of a world would we have? Would it be infused with more nurturing, supportive, caring energy? What difference would it make if those qualities dominated and influenced the structures that create our society? I imagine there would be no more wars. Definitely, there would be lots more pleasure.

This transformation to a better world begins with you. It begins with you and your relationship with your Yoni. Deep in our female bodies are cellular memories of rape, sexual subjugation, beatings, death by birth, domestic violence and lives of unspoken desperation. We hold that history in the cellular memories of our Yonis. We must not forget it has been less than one hundred years since we gained the right to vote. Before that, we didn't have a public voice.

To create a deeper, more reverent relationship with your Yoni, you need to broaden your sexual experiences to include safe, nurturing, trusting, non-agenda and non-goal-oriented touching. This is about re-mapping our sexual experiences as women. If you were sexually abused as a child, then you may have learned that having your personal boundaries crossed and feeling unsafe is part of sexual arousal. Or if you grew up with parents who weren't affectionate with each other, you may have learned that sex takes place behind closed doors. Maybe you learned that sex is not even part of a marriage. Many couples live with sexual anorexia. We may have received many messages from our role models when we were little girls.

How did your mom feel about her Yoni, her sexuality and her body? These messages may have affected what you think about your body, and even what turns you on. Sexuality and sexual arousal is complex and intricate. Your sexuality is as unique as your fingerprint. And each person's sexual needs are different. Honor your needs and the needs of your Yoni by developing greater Yoni Awareness.

YOUR ATTITUDE ABOUT YOUR FEMININE PARTS

What type of attitude do you have about your female genitalia? Do you have kind regard for her and great awareness of her? Do you have pelvic awareness? Is the only pelvic awareness you have called horny? Or do you have another kind of awareness that comes due to a bladder or yeast infection?

Men have a lot of pelvic awareness. Men typically come into a love relationship with lots of awareness in their groins, and women typically come into a relationship with lots of awareness in their hearts. Though women are juicy in their groins too and men open in their hearts, this dynamic of men having more pelvic awareness can leave a woman energetically overwhelmed by his masculine force.

Men are often proud of their genitals. Are you proud of your Yoni? Do you like the way she smells? Do you like the way she looks? Every woman's Yoni is beautiful and uniquely different. Many women, consciously or unconsciously, hold a negative attitude toward their Yonis, thinking it is irregular, misshapen or deformed. This disconnects you from your Yoni.

Knowing how you are disconnected from her is important because most of us don't even realize we are. Some examples of disconnect from your Yoni are what you think about her. If you think she is ugly, then you are disconnected from her. If you don't enjoy having your periods, then you are disconnected from her. If you let someone inside you that you don't really want to let in, you are disconnected from her. If you don't like the way she smells, you are disconnected from her. If you don't clean and wash her with loving kindness, you are disconnected from her. If you douche incessantly, you are disconnected from her. If you indiscriminately and without thought, cut parts of your female reproductive system away, you are definitely disconnected from her.

No matter how far you have strayed from your Yoni and true feminine, she will not stray from you. She will ultimately be true to you by being true to herself. Like a flower, she is of a powerful yet pure essence and doesn't lose her innate wisdom and knowing. A Yoni doesn't lie. If you mistreat her, she will eventually let you know. You may experience pain upon intercourse, fibroids, cramping with periods or other physical symptoms. Your Yoni was designed to feel pleasure. She was designed only to feel this pleasure when she feels safe, nurtured, honored and loved. This is just the way it is. That is why pelvic floor health and self-care of your pelvic bowl and Yoni is extremely important. When you connect to, care for and even stand up for your feminine parts, you will discover your feminine voice. This is the path to reclaiming your true feminine body, not the feminine body our society portrays.

PELVIC FLOOR HEALTH

I like to refer to the pelvic floor as the pelvic bowl. "Floor" signifies flat and strait, whereas "bowl" refers to round, which is more feminine as well as more accurate. The area at the bottom of your body is not a flat board;

it is a bowl. Your pubococcygeus, or PC muscle, is in this bowl. Both men and women have a PC muscle. It is a hammock-like group of muscles that go from the pubic bone to the coccyx bone, your tailbone. This group of muscles forms the pelvic bowl and supports organs in the pelvic cavity.

Some call the PC muscles the love muscles because they are the main muscles that contract when you have an orgasm. If you want to have pelvic floor health and more sexual pleasure, you need to have healthy PC muscles. The PC muscles also cradle, so to speak, our female organs. They also help you maintain balance in your core and create stability in your body, which in turn creates stability in your life.

The muscles in the pelvic floor can hold chronic tension. This is the area of the first and second chakra. The first chakra helps you feel stable and grounded. If you don't feel safe, or if you live with lots of anxiety, then you probably have tension in your pelvic muscles. Healthy muscles expand and contract. They are strong and flexible. When you hold chronic tension, your muscles are in a constant state of contraction. Part of sexual pleasure is letting go, opening up and surrendering. If you hold chronic tension in your pelvic muscles, even if you want to let go, open up and surrender, your body won't let you.

Your feminine parts and your pelvic bowl, when healthy, are similar to a morning glory flower that can both expand and contract. It is important to balance your pelvic bowl. Chronic tension creates a contractive state where there is no space for Spirit to get in. There is no space to let in a higher level of sexual consciousness. You block yourself from letting love into that area. Sexual shame loves to hang out in contractive places in the body. It especially loves to accumulate in our genitals. Nurturing and loving your female anatomy can open these contractive areas and free you of sexual shame.

Infections that create a lack of oxygen to the pelvic bowl can cause a woman to have tense muscles in her pelvic bowl. If you have chronic bladder infections or yeast infections, then you may have built up chronic tension in your pelvic muscles. Also, if you have never ejaculated, don't want to ejaculate because you don't want to make a mess or are ashamed of it, then you may be carrying chronic tension in your pelvic bowl. During sex, ejaculation fluid, or Amrita, builds up. You may hold it in, and not even know it. If you feel embarrassment or shame when you move your hips, or if your hips don't move freely, you may have chronic tension in your pelvic bowl. Negative sexual experiences, unwanted vaginal penetration and unpermitted vaginal entry create chronic tension in the pelvic bowl. If you have been molested, raped or sexually abused and have not experienced sexual healing, then you definitely carry chronic tension in your pelvic bowl.

Pelvic floor health is important. It will help you shift old behavioral patterns and step into your power as a woman. Stepping into your power as a woman is accomplished by putting more loving pleasure into your pelvic bowl. Put more expansive energy "down there" so spirit can get in.

KNOWING WHAT'S "DOWN THERE"

In order to love your Yoni and know your sexual needs, it helps to know what you have "down there." Many women are in the dark as far as knowing what they have. Having a man touch you in a way that "almost" feels good or is hit and miss can be frustrating. How often have men, with a focus of vaginal entry, stimulated the vagina, when what a woman may have preferred was to have her clitoris consciously touched? Or how many men have been lost when trying to find the clitoris? We can't leave it up to our partners to be responsible for knowing our anatomy or our needs. It is important and empowering to take responsibility for our own sexuality and sexual needs, and that includes knowing "what's down there." It is easier for a lover to please a woman when she understands her body.

What *is* down there? To address this subject, I could write another book. It is beyond the scope of this book. However, I would like to provide a brief summary. I also recommend taking a mirror, sitting down in a comfortable place where you have privacy, and looking at yourself. Take a good, long look; get to know yourself. If you want to be an empowered woman and love your body, it is important to know what your Yoni looks like. And remember, your Yoni is as unique as your face. No other woman has a Yoni like yours.

So again, what is down there? You have outer lips and inner lips. You have a clitoris that is more than simply a little button. You have a g-spot and an anterior fornix erogenous (AFE) zone. You also have the ability to ejaculate, somewhat similar to men.

The clitoris, g-spot and AFE zone (or cervix area) are considered the three gates, according to Saida Desilets. The deeper you awaken your Yoni, meaning awaken the first, second and third gates, the deeper you go into yourself, and the deeper the emotional release. For most women, opening the deeper gates requires a deeper level of safety, surrender and emotional intimacy.

Clitoris

The clitoris is not simply a "button." It is much more than that. A whole organ lies under the outer Yoni.

It is easy for women to stay at the first gate, the clitoris, since, for most of us, it is easy to get to, easy to find, and loaded with nerve endings designed for pleasure. It is easy for a woman to believe that's all there is. And the clitoris is powerfully important. It is the only organ in the human body designed for one purpose...pleasure. For example, a man also uses his penis for urination. The clitoris is not simply a "button." It is much more than that. A whole organ lies under the outer Yoni. The visible button part of the clitoris is where the inner lips meet at the top. The unseen part has erectile tissue and "legs" that extend into the body along the pubic bone as much as four to five inches. *Crus* is the singular term, and *crura* is the plural name for the two "legs" of the clitoris that are part of the clitoris' anatomy. The *corpus cavernosum*, *crura* and the *bulb of vestibule* are all erectile tissue that become engorged with blood (similar to a penis) when aroused (see fig 11.9).

THE CLITORIS

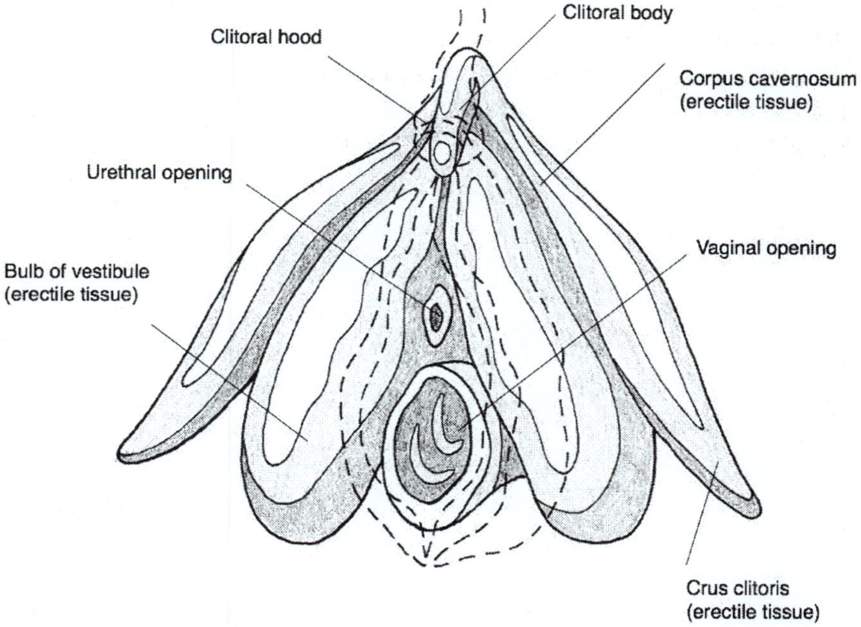

The dotted lines represent what can be seen externally: the clitoral hood and a woman's inner lips (all women's inner lips are unique; this is but an example). The rest of the illustration is the female clitoris. As you can see, it is not just a "button", but a larger organ with erectile tissue.

Figure 11.9

The pudendal nerve innervates the clitoris. I find it interesting that the Latin word *pudent* means, "it shames." Our highly-sensitive erogenous and pleasure zone is rooted in a Latin word meaning shame. No wonder women have had a difficult time cultivating pleasure!

Knowledge is power. Free yourself from this linguistically-rooted shame. Your first gate, your clitoris, is a powerful pleasure tool, which contains more than eight-thousand nerve endings. Its sole function is to have you experience pleasure!

G-Spot

The g-spot, an actual organ that can be stimulated and produce ejaculatory fluid, is the second gate. It is the female prostate gland, and is located on the anterior wall of the vagina. It contains a network of erectile tissues as well as 38 to 40 ducts and glands.

The g-spot is not just a *spot*...it is an actual organ that can be felt and stimulated through the vaginal wall. If you take your tongue and put it on the roof of your mouth right behind your teeth, you will feel a ridged area. The g-spot has a similar ridged area. If you take your finger and put it inside of your vagina, you will feel ridged tissue on the belly side of your vaginal wall. Though it varies from woman to woman, it is not far inside the vagina.

Amrita

Amrita is produced when the g-spot and second gate open. Amrita is Sanskrit for *divine nectar*. It is ejaculatory fluid. Though more women are becoming aware of our ability to ejaculate, many women, when experiencing ejaculation, think they are wetting the bed. This causes embarrassment and shame.

Amrita can vary from a few drops to cups. It can be a forceful stream or not. Both men and woman ejaculate prostatic fluid. The difference is that men's ejaculate contains sperm. When they ejaculate, men can easily lose energy if done too often. For women, it is the opposite. When a woman ejaculates, it renews her. Female ejaculation represents a woman's ability to be comfortable in her masculine side, giving her essence out to the world. On an energetic level, her divine nectar is good for the world. It is part of how she represents herself as an autonomous woman embracing her sexual power.

Due to the way we have made love in the Western world, the g-spot can often be quite numb. All women have the ability to ejaculate. If you don't ejaculate, there is nothing wrong with you. However, if you would like, you can teach yourself how to ejaculate. It may take a fair amount of time and patience to do so. Deborah Sundahl is the author of *Female Ejaculation and the G-spot*. I recommend her book in order to gain a better understanding of your g-spot and the sacred fluid it can produce.

AFE Zone

The AFE zone, or Anterior Fornix Erogenous Zone, also called the A-spot, epicenter or second g-spot, is the third gate. It can also release fluid. It is located on the anterior (belly) side of the vaginal wall, deeper in the vagina near the cervix. Having your cervix consciously massaged and touched can be very arousing. There is not much research regarding the AFE zone since few women have had that area awakened. Saida Desilets talks of a *heartgasm* when this third and deepest gate is awakened. As we become more sexually conscious, i.e., have greater Yoni Awareness, we will awaken the deeper gates. As we do, we will fully embrace our power as women. By the time it is common for women to have an awakened third gate our world will be a different and better place.

As women we are leaders of love. We have medicine for an aching planet. We must first deeply love ourselves, all of ourselves, if we are to lead this world back to a place of love and have peace on earth. This includes loving your private parts and having a sexual relationship with yourself.

SACRED SENSUAL SELF-PLEASURING SESSION

It is important for every woman to create a sexual relationship with herself. We can't rely on having someone in our lives all the time. If you become single and don't have a relationship with your body and your sexuality, you may look outside yourself to fill that need. In doing so, you might attract an unhealthy relationship. A practice of self-pleasuring allows you to fill yourself up so that when you do look for a partner, you are coming from a better place. You won't be starved for affection and "settle."

I don't describe these sessions as *masturbation*. They are sacred sessions for you to create a deeper relationship with your body. This isn't about solely focusing on having an orgasm. This is about exploration, discovery and connection. The session I describe will use a wand. You can also do the session with your hand. However, I have found the wand to be a beneficial tool, and I believe every woman should have one. The one I use and recommend for women is a ten-inch, sensuously curved wand made of crystal Lucite.

You can find them on my website at www.Anna-Thea.com. It has an S-shaped design that gives you the needed leverage to easily reach and stimulate your g-spot, an area that would otherwise be difficult for you to reach and stimulate on your own.

The wand is *not* battery operated. It isn't a vibrator. While I am not completely against vibrators, I believe they are overused, even abused. Vibrators help pre-orgasmic women. Otherwise, they can, if used too aggressively or too often, desensitize instead of re-sensitize the sensitive tissue of your Yoni.

The wand is a powerful tool for any woman who would like to further awaken her feminine sensual aliveness. It can be used as a pleasure tool as well as a pelvic floor health tool. The wand can replace the vibrator and help you tap into the more subtle energies within your Yoni. It can also be used to help you teach yourself how to ejaculate. Also very important, and not as commonly known, it can be used as a healing tool. You can use the wand as a healing tool to nurture, awaken and balance the pelvic floor region and Yoni. It is a powerful tool to release chronic muscle tension and stuck emotions such as fear or sexual shame.

You can use the wand with your beloved or by yourself. I suggest that, in addition to practicing with your beloved, you make dates with yourself. Set aside about an hour, dedicated and uninterrupted, to explore your body and your Yoni with the wand. This is a Sacred Sensual Pleasure session, which cultivates vibrational nourishment.

It is crucial for a woman to experience this rite of passage of pleasuring herself and knowing her body on an intimate level if she is to attract a more aware sexual partner. It would be beneficial if young virgin women learned this before becoming sexual with another. If not, these young women might think of sex as something outside themselves. This thinking can easily set them up for disempowering sexual experiences.

Sacred Sensual Self-pleasuring Session Using the Wand:

Make sure you are clean and that you have emptied your bladder. Lay an absorbent towel down so that it will be under you. This will help keep you from being in your head about peeing or "making a mess." Being in your head will keep you from releasing Amrita (ejaculate), but remember, releasing Amrita is NOT the goal.

To start, lie down with your left hand on your heart and your right hand on your Yoni. Take your time, and become present by taking a few deep breaths. Send energy from your heart down to your Yoni and bless her. You can do this by inhaling, expanding your heart, then exhaling, and sending that heart energy to your Yoni. You can ask for divine guidance for this time with your body. It can be whatever feels best to you, simple prayer, or meditation, to evoke a sense of spiritual connection. It is amazing what a difference a divine meditation or prayer will make in your session.

Surrender to the divine wisdom, take a few deep breaths and start touching your body everywhere except your Yoni. Touch your face, arms and legs. Soft touches, strong squeezes, different types of touches...see what you like. Then relax into it with no agenda. Continue to take deep breaths and make any sounds you would like as you exhale. This will help you get out of your mind and into your body.

Notice what you experience as you touch yourself. Notice what types of touches you enjoy, and which body parts "like" to be touched most. Let your internal dialogue be sweet and caring as you touch your body. Notice if you are being critical and examining. If you are, it means you haven't yet gotten out of your head. Go back to taking more deep breaths. Focus on getting the breath deep into every cell in your body. This will help greatly. The more critical you are, the more deep breathing you will have to do. Allow yourself to enjoy the sensations. After all, *you* are in control.

Then begin to massage the inside of your thighs, the "gateway" to your sexual center and sacred space. The inner thighs are a sexual reflexology area. Three meridians (energy channels), the kidney, spleen and liver meridians, are in this area. It is important to massage your inner thighs in order to open up the sexual energy, open the meridians and let the energy flow. This assists in the release of any emotions, especially fear, anger, worry and guilt that may be bottled up inside you. Then massage as you breathe into all the muscles around the bottom of your body, i.e., the opening of your Yoni, the crease between your Yoni and your legs, and your groin. Let the muscles open and relax.

After you have taken the time to explore, calm your mind and soften into your body through conscious touch, breath, movement and sound, you can begin to use the wand. You can use lubrication if you want or if needed. Coconut oil is excellent for the Yoni, but every Yoni is uniquely different. Find out what your Yoni likes for lubrication. I recommend using something that is natural and doesn't have preservatives or chemical ingredients. Oil nourishes the body. It is often used in Ayurvedic healing practices. Ayurveda is an ancient medical system, from India, for maintaining health.

In Ayurveda, massaging the whole body with oil is called *ambianga*. In this example, you will specifically massage the bottom of the body with oil. This type of massage loosens toxins from your joints and tissues and releases them into your system where they can be eliminated. Oil helps release any accumulated toxins in the skin. It also tones and strengthens the muscles. It increases circulation to the area being massaged, calms the nerve endings and calms the nervous system and mind.

You can insert the wand slowly by exploring on the outside of your Yoni with the wand or a combination of your hand and the wand. Notice the feelings you experience. Take your time as you begin to insert the wand into your Yoni. You may experience some pain, burning or even a feeling that you want to pee. If you have any burning or pain, hold the wand in that location and breathe into it. Going slow and being present with breath awareness allows you to tune in to the more subtle energies of your body. You can experience subtle sensations with very little stimulation, or experience more physical sensations using more energetic movements. Explore combinations of movements, and see what your body responds to.

With the wand, stimulate the front side of your Yoni by pointing the wand upwards, towards your belly. Insert it, and slowly pull it outward, pushing up against the g-spot, almost as if you are milking it. You can also stimulate your clitoris on the outside to create more pleasure. It all depends on how you want to use the wand. A session can be for healing, exploring, processing or releasing old patterns. Other times it can be for orgasmic pleasure and bliss. It can also be a combination of both. See what your body enjoys. It may be different each time or similar. The important thing is to get to know your femininity on an intimate level. Remember that the session doesn't have to have the goal of reaching orgasm or ejaculation. This session is for YOU to get to know, on a deeper level, your unique sexual imprint. Use your intuition and divine guidance, and let it unfold.

If you want to teach yourself how to ejaculate with the wand, here are some helpful guidelines.

- Invoke sacred space and ask for divine guidance when you begin the session.
- Make sure you allow at least an hour of uninterrupted time for yourself.
- Have *no agenda* to accomplish ejaculation, but rather to simply explore.
- Treat your Yoni and your body with extreme kindness and love.
- Breathe…deeply.
- Squeeze your PC muscle.

- Allow deep sounds from your throat.
- Hold your breath for a few seconds at the top or bottom of the breath.
- Bear down or push.
- Let go and simply open to the experience.

Your relationship with your body will be unique. It is a journey, not a destination. Enjoy the journey. Support yourself in blossoming to your full feminine potential. This can mean teaching yourself to ejaculate or not. You are the leader of your helm. Make the intimate relationship you create with yourself one of loving presence with no agenda to "get somewhere." Let this sacred, sensual, self-pleasuring session be only a guide. The rest is up to you to create what you want in regards to a loving relationship with yourself and your body. Be creative. Be explorative. Be sensual. Be nurturing. Be loving. The main point is to take the time and do it.

EXERCISE:

In this chapter, you discovered many ways to put more love into your sexuality. What resonated most with you? What practices and/or principles can you implement starting TODAY? List five things you are willing to do to put more love into your sexuality.

1.____

2.____

3.____

4.____

5.____

CONCLUSION

Commit to Yourself

Commitment is how you grow and evolve
It increases your self-esteem and heightens your resolve
Creating a life of love, intimacy and deep connection
Takes effort, commitment and focused intention
It brings clarity to your life and radiance to your being
No longer having to go along, get along and always agreeing
Your feminine potency, purpose and passion
Will arouse in you tremendous penetrating compassion
Knowing that your essence is vast and strong
Frees you from shame and thinking you're wrong
Instead you become succulent, juicy and authentically attractive
No longer having to be a "masculine adaptive"
Through commitment you step into an influential place
That allows you to live your life in pure feminine grace
Opening to the gift of your true feminine essence
Gives you an extremely potent and powerful presence
Commitment is how you grow and evolve
It increases your self-esteem and heightens your resolve.

You hold within you the seed to create peace on our beautiful planet. Now that you have read this book, you know more about the power you hold within. You understand the benefits of getting out of your mind and being present in your body. You have discovered ways to create a love relationship with food. You have received ideas on how to have a love affair with your body. And you have learned how to put more love into your sexuality.

Are you willing to commit to empowering yourself by loving your body for the rest of your life? We grow and evolve through commitment. When you make a commitment, you create inner strength and become more effective in the world. When you are committed to something, you're less likely to give up or feel defeated when you face a challenge or something you don't understand. You know where you're going and what you're moving towards. Nothing slows you down. You live life more passionately, and you become more attractive to others. You become a beacon of light as you shine your brightness out into the world. When you commit to yourself, you feel worthy. You empower yourself through commitment.

Are you ready to commit to yourself and the blossoming of your authentic feminine? I am challenging you to take action. Now is the time to deeply love and honor yourself even more. What actions are you going to take to do so? What coaches, mentors or guidance will you seek to embrace your inner feminine?

This book has given you many tools and provided knowledge. You will only benefit from this information if you take action. Knowledge becomes power when it is applied and experienced; then it becomes wisdom. I am calling to you to claim your authentic feminine power and embrace your feminine wisdom. Become the leader of love you are meant to be, and start today, not tomorrow.

Your feminine body is a powerful channel, a vessel of divine love. Having a love relationship with food, a love affair with your body and putting more love into your sexuality opens your vessel to more of this never-ending source of divine love. Are you fully ready to embody this divine love?

I invite you to take five minutes and write, in the five lines provided below, what you can do immediately to empower your feminine self. List the top five actions you can take to create a better you within the next 90 days. Maybe it is paying attention to your inner dialogue or something even more challenging like facing a long-standing issue that you haven't wanted to face. Maybe it is committing to a yoga practice or dancing with abandon for ten minutes in your house every day. Or maybe it is attending a workshop, online course or buying one of my feminine empowering products. Maybe it is investing in yourself by hiring a coach, finding a mentor or joining a group.

Perhaps one of these action steps is to go back through the book and complete the exercises at the end of each chapter. This book is your tool, your support to help you empower yourself by loving your body. Let it be your journal, let it be your guide.

NOTE: I encourage you to complete the exercises at the end of each chapter, the page numbers of the exercises are as follows: 45, 67, 107, 188, and 232.

EXERCISE:

I commit to loving myself and empowering myself by...

1. ______________________________
2. ______________________________
3. ______________________________
4. ______________________________
5. ______________________________

A Final Note

In this book, you learned many ways to deeply love and honor yourself. You learned about being present in your body and working with your emotions in a productive way. You learned about creating a loving relationship with food and your body. You learned about the importance of holding your sexuality as sacred and shifting your attitude about your femininity.

Now that you have read the book, I encourage you to contact me. I would love to hear what you enjoyed most about the book and how I can improve it in future editions. Most of all, I would like to hear from you. I would like to hear about your challenges, your fears, your struggles and your heartaches. Tell me about your journey of intimacy. Let me know how I can help you. I am available for a phone conversation. I am also available to do a private workshop or talk in your area.

I would like to offer you a no-obligation, complimentary 30-60 minute consultation to help empower you as a woman. My cell number is 702-306-3984, and my email address is glowbal2@gmail.com. Due to spam, it is better to text instead of email. I can also be reached on Facebook at www.facebook.com/annatheafab. Please include your name and time zone to facilitate coordinating your complimentary phone (or Skype) consultation.

Let the end of this book be a new beginning for you. Take what you have read and apply it to your life and your relationships, including the relationship you have with yourself. May your journey be blessed with much pleasure, joy and love!

Your friend,

Anna-Thea

About the Author

Anna-Thea is an author, speaker and intimacy coach. Her heartwarming and inspiring teachings, filled with wisdom, will open your heart. As an intimacy coach, she is dedicated to helping women live more sensually aware lives and speak confidently from their hearts. Anna-Thea offers practical and loving solutions for women with food issues, body image issues, relationship, intimacy and/or sexual issues.

Anna-Thea has a degree in dietetics, graduating with honors. In 1997, Yoga became her passion. She is a Level 2 certified Kundalini Yoga and Vinyasa Flow instructor. Her most valuable education came from the Divine Feminine Institute, where she received a double certification as a Spiritual Sexual Educator and a Divine Feminine Educator. Using principles from her extensive studies in yoga, nutrition, psychology and the Divine Feminine Institute, she coaches women on developing their authentic feminine confidence. She offers workshops, speaking engagements and individual coaching. Her workshops, educational products and presentations are fun, powerfully educational and experientially transforming.

She lived in Las Vegas, Nevada, for 19 years, though she is originally from the San Francisco Bay Area. She currently lives in the beautiful foothills of the Sierra Nevada mountains in Northern California.

About Anna-Thea's Blog

Anna-Thea's Body Wisdom offers inspiration and wisdom for women.

When you sign up for her blog, you will receive, each week, a short article or a link to a short video that provides uplifting information about the beauty, magic and wonder of your body as a woman. We hold the mysteries, and too often we hold them from ourselves. Anna-Thea's blog helps you have a greater understanding, reverence and appreciation for the powerful feminine essence that you hold within you.

When you sign up, you will receive two gifts:

1. An ebook, "Seven Secrets to Deeply Love and Honor Your Body."

2. An 11-minute guided meditation. It will leave you feeling relaxed and renewed. It is a powerful tool for releasing stress when your life gets hectic or to use as a daily practice.

Sign up for Anna-Thea's blog at:

www.Anna-Thea.com or
www.EmpowerYourselfByLovingYourBody.com

Personal Coaching with Anna-Thea

Are you tired of obsessing about food, your body or relationships? Would you like to feel more sensually alive and in your power as a woman? Would you like to have the clarity and confidence to speak your truth in emotionally charged situations and not damage relationships due to emotional outbursts? Would you like to fully embrace your femininity instead of fear it?

For more than 25 years, Anna-Thea has helped thousands of women live in their feminine strength and confidence. She can help you, too. She provides one-on-one coaching via Skype or phone, and you can be part of her community to support you to your next level of reclaiming your body and your authentic power as a woman.

For a complimentary, no-obligation, 30-60 minute consultation by phone or Skype, call or text the number below.

Let Anna-Thea support you in being all that you can be!

www.Anna-Thea.com
www.EmpowerYourselfByLovingYourBody.com
glowbal2@gmail.com
702-306-3984

Book Anna-Thea to Speak at Your Next Event

When it comes to choosing a professional speaker for your next event, you will find no one more inspiring and thought-provoking than Anna-Thea. She is a talented speaker who brings entertainment, education, laughter and deep emotion into the experience for your group. Participants will leave the presentation feeling inspired, empowered and extremely thankful to you for having chosen Anna-Thea to speak at the event. Whether your audience is 20 or 20,000, in the United States or abroad, Anna-Thea offers a powerful message for women that can be tailored to fit the theme of your event. Anna-Thea's wish is to inspire and ignite a renewed sense of passion in your audience through sharing her personal experiences and feminine wisdom to create transformation for your participants. If you are looking for a dynamic, heart-centered speaker who will leave your audience wanting more, book Anna-Thea today. To see a highlight video of Anna-Thea and inquire about her availability for your next meeting, conference or event, visit her website at the address below. Then contact her by phone or email to schedule a complimentary pre-speech phone interview.

www.Anna-Thea.com
www.EmpowerYourselfByLovingYourBody.com
glowbal2@gmail.com
702-306-3984

Printed in Great Britain
by Amazon

36338749R00142